CHAKRAS, MYTHOLOGY and ASTROLOGICAL SYMBOLISM

Johnny Barnett

Chakras, Mythology and Astrological Symbolism
by Johnny Barnett
www.chakraology.org

© 2018 Johnny Barnett

Design by Anna Magruder
Cover illustration by Johann Georg Gichtel (1638-1710)
Edited by Lesley Carmody and Anna Magruder

ISBN-13: 978-1718718098
ISBN-10: 1718718098

First Edition

PREFACE

This book is a direct outgrowth of the 2-hour class "Chakras, Mythology and Astrological Symbolism" which I have been presenting live for 7 years. Last year, one of my hosts pointed out that I had too much information to fit into two hours and so this book was born. What follows is a compilation of centuries of fact, mythology, religion, history, esoteric thought and Spiritual truths handed down through the ages of our Western culture. Very little of what I offer here is original material – the newness perhaps lies in my arranging of the material in a certain fashion, coupled with the hindsight that is afforded one living in the 21st century.

The genesis of the class lies in a handful of conversations I had in the mid-2000's with other Spiritually-minded folks in my community in Austin, Texas. As the only practicing astrologer in our circle, I was often posed with astrological questions. And as yoga, meditation and words like "Chakra" became more prevalent in our culture, the question on everyone's mind was, "What is the relationship between the planets and the Chakras?" We had the easy and obvious correspondence between the 7 Chakras and the 7 colors of the rainbow. Other 7s appear throughout the ancient and medieval world – 7 Seas, 7 Hills of Rome, 7 Deadly Sins, 7 Days of Creation, etc., and the idea that they were all related in corresponding fashion – just as the colors are to the Chakras – was intriguing.

How to match the 10 planets of modern astrology with only 7 Chakras, however, was a puzzle. Try as I might I could not comfortably eliminate 3 planets just to make it "fit" the mold. Eventually I filed this question in the back of my mind as other more pressing matters (family) took priority in my life.

Then, one day in the winter of 2011 – my son having graduated high school and moved out – I stumbled upon the work of a sound healer who corresponded the 7 white notes of the piano with the 7 Chakras. There it was again! That ubiquitous number 7 and its presence – not only in the esoteric world, but also in the common, everyday world. And as I began to re-count all the 7s I knew of – continents on the earth, colors of the rainbow, days of the week, lucky 7s on each of the opposing sides of dice – I finally recalled the 7 planets in that 'other' astrological system – Vedic. The "aha moment" of my career! The 7 in Vedic are the same 7 in Classic Western astrology; we in the West just added the outer 3 planets once they were 'discovered'. The 7 as I recalled are visible to the naked eye, but the outer 3 required a telescope to see. Another aha! (I later came to understand these outer 3 planets to be significantly different in their role in one's astrological chart – but that is another book.) The 7 visible planets, I realized, represent *embodied* forces or Chakras.

CONTENTS

ACKNOWLEDGMENTS

My gratitude goes out to all the people who have helped to bring this book into being:

First, to all my previous hosts and hostesses who have given me the space and support to present the class that this book is based upon. Second, to the friends who have been my biggest fans along the way – Mary, Tej, Sunisa, Graell, Andrew, everyone at the A.R.E., Krista, Donna, David and Zen.

Brennyn for 11th hour consultations

Lesley Carmody for editing

Anna Magruder for editing, layout, artwork, long hours and brilliant brainstorming

to Alex for introducing me to the art of Astrology

to Terra for hosting the first-ever class

and to Dawn-Marie for saying just what I needed to hear to convince me to write this book.

INTRODUCTION

This book is for you. Even if you know nothing about astrology or chakras, the words in this book will make sense because it is the story of Life, which we are all experiencing. Esoteric topics like astrology and chakras simply give us a language to express that which we are feeling and knowing to be true, so you will easily understand these following pages because it is your story. Easy and familiar and yet you may have never heard these ideas discussed or expressed exactly this way. These ideas having been hidden by the wise, ignored by science and vilified by organized religion through the last several centuries – preachers, teachers and parents typically know little to nothing about the powerful Spiritual and biological motivations that underlie the actions of human beings. So here you will find answers to big questions – most notably, "Why am I here?" – unencumbered by religious dogma, cultural 'norms' or parental bias. And due to the fact that most, if not all, great literature – from the fairy tales you grew up with, to the classic works of Shakespeare to the 7 Harry Potter books – is a re-telling of this same theme, and so has been in your awareness and your culture since you were born, you will find yourself saying, "Oh yeah, of course!" as you read, more often than, "Huh?"

Chakraology – the word I coined in 2011 to describe my work – is the study of the interplay between Spirit and Matter. The Radiance Sutras express this notion most eloquently – "Within this very body are many gateways to the Infinite, where Incarnation and Immortality consummate their passion for each other".[1] That is a large part of the underlying thesis of this book – that you are actually a combination of Spirit and Matter and that – far from being secondary (as some religions will try and tell you) – your physical body is in fact an essential component of your reason for being, and that your Purpose cannot be achieved without it. In other words – Spirit needs Matter (your body) just as much as the body needs consciousness to animate it. And so these 7 Chakras become the "gateways" – the places where Spirit 'comes through' and enters the physical world. This is also reflected in the notion that "one does not live Life; rather Life (spirit) is living you".

A closely related idea which is so ancient that you may have not heard it before is that the 7 Planets outside of us are a representation of the 7 energy centers or Chakras inside of us. The saying "As above, so below" is a decent rendering of this concept. A better saying is "As *without*, so *within*". So you will see words for specific planets and their corresponding Chakras – the planet Mars and the Root Chakra for example – used interchangeably throughout this book. You may have already noticed the picture on the cover showing a man with the planetary symbols inside of his Chakras – a drawing from 17th Century Europe made by a Bavarian Alchemist named Johann Gichtel. The fact that (at least some) Europeans knew about Chakras almost 400 years ago while most of us in the United States have only become aware of them in the last 20 years or so will, I hope, begin to open your mind to the idea that there is much more going on inside of and around you than you have been led to believe.

It is my belief that our cultural predisposition to focus upon the physicality of life and to relegate the Spiritual side of life to the back-burner, to be called upon and considered only in times of great loss, grief or challenge, has left us handicapped – moving through life with only half the picture to guide us, not knowing that the other half (spirit) provides the impetus, the drive and motivation that make us 'go'. It's like driving a car without knowing there is an engine making it move. It's under the hood where we can't see it so we just don't think about it as naturally as we think about the traffic and the signs and the lines on the road. We do have a gauge to remind us there is an engine that needs attention (gas, oil, etc.) but these realities only thrust themselves upon us when they are in a critical stage of depletion. Likewise, Spiritual awareness appears for the most part to be optional – something we can get along without paying much or any attention to.

And so it is – consciousness is optional indeed. We may resist the awareness of our Spiritual nature just as we may resist any other concept or fact that rubs us the wrong way, upsets us or contradicts our beliefs. Cognitive Dissonance is a well-documented fact of human nature.

This book then is intended for those who wish to embrace their true nature and understand more fully the interplay between Spirit and Matter in our lives, which will help you understand more fully yourself and the people around you. We will journey far beyond the clichéd pick-up line "What's your sign?" to a deeper level of understanding as we glimpse the powerful forces (Chakras) that are related to these signs via the *planets* that rule these signs. These 7 planets are an exterior representation of an interior reality – the 7 Chakras. Patterns that you have seen in your family and friends will start to make sense even if you know nothing about astrology. For those who do know something of astrology this book will add to your astrological tool-box and give you a new way to look at birth charts and help your friends and clients. And for those desiring to keep their Chakras operating smoothly, you will gain some insight as to how they can get out of balance and what you may do to address it.

This book is the written version of my 2-hour class "Chakras, Mythology and Astrological Symbolism". Before beginning each class, and here as well, I offer a few key points so you will hopefully not mistake this book for a religious one even when you see the word "God" or examples from the Bible.

The Bible as it turns out is actually written on many levels. Beyond the literal vs. metaphorical interpretations that most of us have heard debated, there is at least one other way to read the Bible and that is by reading the code that lies within the words. Similar to *The DaVinci Code* where we were shown the messages encoded in the art of Leonardo Da Vinci – there are meanings hidden in plain sight if you have "eyes to see them".[2] Even Jesus himself alluded to these hidden messages and so this book will bring a few of those hidden gems to light. The particular code I am referring to is of course related to the Chakras and we will see its evidence in the upcoming chapters.

Now, the word "God" is probably the most dangerous word we have and so a brief explanation of what is meant and what is not meant when I use the word "God" is in order. First off, I, and many of you perhaps, grew up using the word "God" as a name. It was the name of the Supreme Being, the Creator of the Universe, the Father – the all-powerful being who lived in a place called "heaven". God was an actual *person*. That is to say – a being with emotions, preferences, judgments – a *personality*. Supernatural, omniscient, divine perhaps – and yet a person. God had a gender (male). "He" referred to "Himself" in the first *person*. As a Christian child I was taught not to say "goddamn" because I was "taking the Lord's *name* in vain". So "God's" name, I was taught, was – God.

I believe this is one of the prime fallacies that lie at the heart of Judeo/Christian culture – the notion that "God" is a personal being (and "Heaven" a physical place.) My use of this word is quite different. In our world I see a clear distinction between 'Spirit' and 'Matter'. Matter refers to 'things' – stuff that can be seen, heard, smelled, tasted and/or touched. Spirit is every-*thing* else. (More about things that are not things in chapter 4). Thoughts, feelings, energy, consciousness, spirit are all non-physical or non-material parts of our life – very real indeed but you can't hear a feeling, you can only *feel* it. And so I will use the word "God" interchangeably with words like "Spirit", "Energy", "Source", "The Universe" and "The Cosmos". You may envision any thing or person you like when you read the word "God" in these pages and this book will work just fine and should make perfect sense to you. Just know that this is not a religious book and God, to this author, is something quite different than what you may be taught in church.

In fact, I will refer to Jesus and Moses in the same way I refer to the gods of mythology – that is to say – as characters who symbolize certain energies and facets of life rather than as real people. You may believe that Jesus and Moses existed (and I personally hope that they did), but the fact is, no one in living memory has interacted with these men personally. No one really knows what was said and done thousands of years ago and unless you were there you don't even know what was really said and done in the White House, the Governor's Mansion or the Kremlin yesterday. And so the Bible stories are considered in this book in the same light as Myths – profound stories designed to illustrate the important aspects of living with lessons, guidance and examples of what occurs when you are true to your human nature.

A note on mythology; the Greeks are credited with creating Western mythology. The Romans, after having conquered the Greeks, changed the names of the Greek gods to fit their language. And so we are left with the names Jupiter, Mars, Saturn, Venus and Mercury even though the stories most of our subsequent cultural references (and this book) are based upon are the stories of Zeus, Ares, Cronos, Aphrodite, and Hermes.

In the esoteric view, as well as that of physics, our Universe is dualistic, comprised of Spirit (or energy if you prefer) and Matter. Everything in the physical/dualistic world is known by its opposite. Up does not exist without Down. Left has no meaning without reference to Right. Male/

Female, Light/Dark, North/South, etc. God then, is conceptually spirit and its physical counterpart or opposite is Matter – conceptualized as "the Earth". Human Beings then exist as the combination of the two – spirit housed within matter – your eternal spirit encased in your mortal body here on planet Earth. At this point the word "God" stands for something entirely different. As spirit, God loses gender, name and personality. If anything God can be likened to a *presence* or a *force* that exists. That *is*. "I am that I am" is said in the Bible to be the "name of god". I believe this is an ancient expression of the notion of God as a word that describes the "presence" that is. Everywhere. A part of Everything. The 'thing' that exists everywhere but is not a *physical thing* but a *Spiritual presence*.

So I will be dropping the word "God" from time to time in these pages as well as quoting from the Bible. Astrology and many other esoteric traditions promote the notion of an individual being able to experience this presence without having to go through an intermediary like a church or religion – of having a direct link or contact with your Source. Religions, like governments, are comprised of people – some doing their best to uphold the principles of Godliness or promote the presence of spirit in a material world, and others who are not. So with this book I hope you may gain an insight into the presence of God/ spirit on your own – without the potentially corrupting influence of religious persons. Of course you may be influenced by ME – but as I have yet to become rich, famous or unduly powerful, it is likely that I have become less corrupted than your average preacher or senator. Be that as it may I ask that you do not 'believe' a single word

I have written. Rather, I suggest you take the information here and see if it fits. Decide for yourself whether the words you find in these pages to be true, useful or worthy of remembering. Someone once pointed out that one of the most powerful revisions to the first draft of the Declaration of Independence was the insertion of the phrase "self evident" as in – "We hold these truths to be self-evident". So too, I believe the truths within this book to be self-evident. Perhaps you will find them to be so as well.

Johnny Barnett
March, 2018
Taos, NM

Chapter 1

ROOT CHAKRA – MARS

"I am Here..."

Our Spiritual journey and purpose begin firmly rooted in the Physical experience. This paradox underlies the entirety of our existence, which will become more and more apparent as we journey through the chakras. As you journey into this book, that your Spiritual purpose is directly tied to your Physical being becomes apparent. Some religions and many Spiritual–minded folks will pooh-pooh the physical side of life. Statements such as "Your reward is in Heaven" or "I am a Spiritual being having a physical experience" may or may not be true but they are mostly attempts at minimizing the physical side of life while uplifting the Spiritual, and often providing justification for oneself or others not being rich, healthy, or materially successful. I would change that Spiritual bumper sticker to read "I am a Spiritual Being *and* a Physical Being" Now. Here and Now. Your true nature may be Spiritual and your presence on the earth in this body may indeed be temporary but it is my belief that this time spent here and now, in the body, is very important and quite purposeful.

So we start at the Root Chakra which is essentially concerned with existing and surviving in the physical dimension – or in other words – staying alive. Just as a plant has a literal root that connects it to the Earth – and if you pull it out by the root it will die – so too, our Root Chakra symbolizes our connection to the Earth or, our life. The question of whether there is life after death is easily answered by the Root Chakra – certainly not! Your Physical life begins with your birth and ends with your death. At which point some *part* of you may experience the *afterlife*, but *you* – the person you are at this moment, with this name, personality, family history and body, and existing at this time – will only be here once.

The word reincarnation means to incarnate again – a new incarnation for your spirit in a new body, obviously in a new time (if not place). And though soul-groups are said to incarnate together multiple times, the relationships, identities, bodies and personalities are never all the same. There is only one *you* and you are Here. Now.

ROOT ISSUES

Food. Clothing. Shelter. These, we are told, are the bare necessities of life. These needs tend to overshadow the rest of your experience when they are not getting met. Have you ever lost your temper, broken traffic laws or ignored other's needs when you were really, really hungry? Have you ever tried to work when you were sick? Have you ever felt like *doing* anything when you were in a hospital, immediately after surgery, or when a loved-one was facing a life-threatening situation? Taking care of the body is the first thing that must happen before we are able to entertain any other type of thought or activity. Spirit needs you to stay in the body in as good a condition as possible for as long as you are *here*. Rest also needs mentioning. As one of the "3 Pillars of Life" from the Vedic tradition, Rest ranks up there with Food, Clothing and Shelter. You sleep (almost) every night. Your body needs to recharge. You may have often heard a young parent saying their baby is cranky because they didn't get their nap. You need your nap too! You will be just as cranky and insufferable as that baby if you don't get the proper amount of rest you need.

WORK

Your spirit – having incarnated into your body – is now earth-bound. Rooted, as it were, in your body. And so the body – its care, condition and survival are the primary focus of spirit operating through the Root Chakra. Food, clothing and shelter lead us to money – as almost none of us in the West grow all of our food, make all of our clothes and build our own houses. Money is a means for survival (in Jazz lingo and other slang, the word "bread" means money.) Therefore what you do to get money becomes an integral expression of your being.

Our planetary companion to the 1st Chakra is the god Mars, who is primarily a '*do-er*'. Action. Physical Activity. Movement. The question, "What do you *do* for a *living*?" is the essential Root Chakra question. We all must do something to either earn the money needed for living or otherwise we spend our physical energy growing or hunting food, making clothes and building/maintaining our home. Either way you must *do* something. Even the stay at home moms and dads are "doing" plenty. Even though they may not be paid in money they are still working to ensure the survival of the members of the family – feeding, cleaning, and cooking are all necessary for survival.

Often other languages give us valuable clues to the deeper layers of meaning that can be often lacking in our current use of English. In Spanish, the question, "What is your work?" or, "What is your job?" translates into, "A que tu dedicas?" or literally, "To what are you *dedicated*?". To what are you dedicating your life's energy and time? Your work takes on a whole new significance when you realize that you are given a finite amount of time to be *here* and a degree of health that may at any time be suddenly decreased by accident or illness. Instead of simply having a J-O-B that you are not intimately attached to or perhaps even hate – your WORK can be seen as the result of a powerful choice you have made as to how you will *spend* your life's energy.

Mozart's "body of work" is his music. A legacy that has endured beyond his physical existence. It is almost impossible to think of Mozart as hating to go to work. So too, when we discover something worth our time and energy we may dedicate our lives to it. And in so doing you may yourself leave a legacy behind.

SEX

Speaking of legacies, our children are a physical

legacy – that of our physical genetics surviving in another generation. Our sexuality therefore, has its root in our biological need to reproduce – a need shared by every plant and animal on Earth. Your sexuality may extend beyond this biological urge, and we will be looking at it more in future chapters, but sexuality begins at the Root Chakra and the desire to reproduce.

Now not everyone will reproduce. And many will say, "I don't want to have children" or, "I am not ready to have children yet" or, "I choose to adopt rather than have my own children". And at the same time this urge to reproduce – most often referred to as the "biological clock" – is there. And it is powerful. In fact, like all survival instincts it is among the most powerful physical urges we experience. And it exists for men as well as women. Straight and gay. A glance at the latest published statistics of unplanned pregnancies or an informal poll of you, your siblings, co-workers and friends will quickly reveal that around half of us came into this world unexpectedly.

In fact even as you read this sentence another unplanned child is being conceived. And how many unplanned children do you think will have been born by the time you finish this chapter? The point is, no matter what you may "think" about having children, the biological urge to reproduce may rise up and dominate your being at a certain point (or several) in your life.

Our Root Chakra issues – health, vitality, survival – can at times override other elements of our life such as decisions, thoughts, values, religious beliefs and so on. Typically when we are drunk, high, grieving, falling in love – experiencing emotional extremes or being taken "out of our mind" by substances – we find we are more likely to "do" things that we wouldn't otherwise do. As the great musician and cynic John Lennon once said, "Most of us are born out of a whiskey bottle".

In the Vedic tradition of ancient India the 3 "Pillars of Life" are rest, digestion and managing your sexual energy – a term almost no one in the West has heard uttered by parents, friends or counselors. Managing your sexual energy begins with understanding that your biological urges have a way of dominating your experience from time to time and therefore the wise person will not take them lightly. "Just say no" is not a management strategy. Knowing you have at times the overpowering urge to reproduce and then deciding how you wish to handle it is the beginning of a management strategy.

WAR

Our biological urges cover far more than just sex. Our needs for food, clothing and shelter are just as strong. It is very difficult to maintain a Spiritual disposition or subscribe to a high-minded philosophy when you are starving to death. In the 20th century we were told "poverty breeds violence". That is to say – almost every human being will resort to stealing if they are faced with the choice to either steal or starve to death.

Mars in mythology is the God of War. Wars – for the most part – are fought for economic and other resource-related reasons (fertile farmland, abundant hunting grounds, access to fresh water or the ocean, raw materials such as minerals, timber and oil). If you think there are other motives for starting a war I encourage you to read "War is a Racket" written by Maj. General Smedley Butler – the most highly decorated US Marine of his time – who tells us that his entire military career was dedicated to fighting around the globe on behalf of corporate interests.

WARRIORHOOD

Warriorhood, in its traditional meaning is representative of something more palatable than war. In earlier centuries and other cultures where physical survival was/is an uncertain thing, Warriors are developed and trained to defend all those who are unable to defend themselves. Typically, this was exclusively a male role as almost all men are physically stronger than almost all women and therefore better able to successfully defend the keys to survival – the women and children. In fact, here in the US, women have only recently been allowed to serve in the Armed Forces in combat roles due mainly to the fact that we in the US no longer consider ourselves to be under threat of extinction from foreign enemies and so (a relatively few) women are now considered as expendable as men. This was not the case before the fall of the Soviet Union, which up to that point was considered a very real threat to completely annihilate the United States.

Going back to our definition of Warrior as one who is stronger and better able to defend those who are weaker – we realize that everyone is stronger than someone at some point in time, and Warriorhood is a role we all may play – women, men and children. Take any mother whose child may, for example, be suddenly at risk from an aggressive dog at the park. This woman will immediately shift into warrior mode – her fight or flight response kicks in, her adrenals begin pumping, her heart rate goes up, her entire focus of body and mind is upon that dog and what she must do to protect her child. And rest assured – no matter what her upbringing or beliefs or size – she will do *anything* needed to protect that child.

The child will also one day be in a situation where he or she can help a friend who has hurt themself, or a classmate who is being bullied. The best example of this concept of Warrior as protector comes to us from the film "Hook" in which Robin Williams plays the adult Peter Pan. At the end of the film when Captain Hook has been vanquished and Peter must return to the 'real' world, he is debating on which of the Lost Boys he should leave in charge. His beautiful and heart-warming solution is to select the biggest boy and then say to him "Take care of everyone smaller than you."[3] This is our job as Warriors, as human beings – to defend and protect those whom we can.

SERVICE

One of the main benefits of a matriarchal culture – or at very least the honoring and veneration of women by men – is that it keeps the Martian energy in check. Mars is housed in the Root Chakra – the base or bottom of the system. It is there at the bottom so it may support the rest of the system. When your physical needs and urges are dominating rather than serving the rest of your life, you are thrown off balance just as when the military becomes more powerful than the rest of the government and the country is thrown out of balance. To avoid this, the Founding Fathers of the United States set up the constitution so that the President, elected by the people, would be the military Commander-in-Chief – rather than the biggest and most powerful general. In ancient Rome, military commanders were not allowed to bring their armies into the city – or in other words – to threaten the government. Caesar's crossing of the Rubicon – the river that ran outside of Rome – was a sign that the military was taking over. And history shows us just how well that worked out for Caesar and Rome.

So too, our own Mars must be in service to the rest of our chakras just as our military personnel must be in service to the country, our police in service to the public, and the strong in service to the weak. Any strong person who is not using their physical strength in service to a higher principle will sooner or later become a bully – whether it is a child, a husband or a police officer. And if your sex-drive or drive to succeed and survive are not kept in check by your higher (literally, higher up the chakra system) ideals, we become slaves to our own Mars – behaving like greedy children.

THE HERO

Firefighters – those guys who race around town in red trucks – are modern-day Warriors, risking their lives to protect those in need. Have you ever been close to a firefighter? These guys (and gals) are huge. Big muscles. You have to be strong in order to handle heavy water hoses and save people from burning buildings. Strength, endurance and a large dose of adrenaline must be on tap for whenever needed. Not everyone fits the bill for becoming a professional Warrior, though everyone can be an amateur. In fact all of our stories with Heroes in them are designed to evoke the Warrior within each of us. The Hero must face a daunting challenge, find the strength needed from within and push through to the other side – slay the monster, vanquish the enemy, blow up the Death Star, save the town from a gang of marauding bandits, etc. Strength, will, adrenaline and stamina are all focused upon the task. Without this concentration of force the attempt will not succeed. The symbol for Mars includes a very sharp pointed spear symbolizing this focus and drive to push through a challenge. You may have also noticed this symbol on the Men's Room door. It represents amongst other things the Penis – that physical part of a man which enacts the masculine principle of penetration.

MORE SEX

Penetration is actually the energetic beginning (1st Chakra) to everything. The sperm must penetrate the egg to initiate conception. The Biblical story of creation (which occurs in the "1st" book) is esoterically read as the masculine principle – Spirit/God – penetrating the feminine principle – Matter/Earth. Penetration of the Feminine by the Masculine is the most dynamic process in the Universe – the process by which Creativity is enabled. The other element in the symbol for Mars is the circle.

Paired with the Spear we have a representation of the

penetrator and the *penetratee* – penis and vagina. And so the act of Penetration – vagina penetrated by penis, egg penetrated by sperm – relates to the beginning of our physical conception, the beginning of our creation myth and the beginning of our Chakra System. Remember from the start of this chapter – our first three words are "I am here". And the way we get here is via the act of penetration. Your Spirit also penetrated the Matter of your body at some point in your gestation. A quick view of the location of the 1st Chakra shows its proximity to the genitals.

DRIVE

Penetration, however, extends far beyond the physical acts of sex or sperm/egg. If you are going to a meeting for example, you walk into the meeting room through the door. (Notice how the word *door* has the letter 'o' – similar to the feminine part of the Mars symbol?) You have penetrated the room. Now and only now can the meeting begin. But you do have to get through the door first. You have to engage your will and your muscles to walk through that door. Mars is that drive to get what you want and it ranges all the way from going to the other side of the room to get a drink of water, to pursuing your goals and ambitions with single-minded intensity and drive until you reach them. Assertion is the hallmark of a healthy Root Chakra. Assertion is the penetration of your will into the dynamic of a situation. This is what I want; this is what I say. It is neither inherently positive or negative, simply the expression of one's will. *Aggression* is Martian assertion taken a step further – attempting to force one's will upon others, while *submission* is the absence of Martian energy – the path to slavery, just as aggression is the path to dominance. But assertion – simply showing up as a unique personality with unique gifts, desires and points of view – is what we are designed to do.

LOOKING OUT FOR #1

One of the most telling features of the energy of the Root Chakra is its number – 1. The number '1' and the letter 'I' are almost the exact same character. When it comes to our sexuality the Root Chakra symbolizes our own personal sexual needs – What do I need? How often do I need it? Who do I like to sleep with (men/ women)?

Venus and the 2nd Chakra are where we actually *relate* to other people, but down in the Root our 1st concern is our own needs and getting them met.

The cultural archetype who best symbolizes Mars in all its glory is James Bond. He's a warrior, a company man and a sex-machine. How many women does James Bond get? All of them. How many does he love? None of them. As a character operating solely from his Root Chakra he is not capable of Love. He is only concerned with his survival, the carrying out of his 'job' and getting his own sexual needs met. He's looking out for #1. Seen in a different context the quality of looking out for yourself is not such a terrible thing. For all the helpers, healers, martyrs and professional "do-gooders" reading this book – and who may object to relating in any way shape or form to the example of James Bond – I must point out that anyone traveling on a commercial airliner will be told point blank – in an emergency – take care of your own needs first. Put that oxygen mask on yourself before you try and put one on your child. You will be no use to anyone if you are passed out unconscious. In fact you will become an additional burden to others. We all must look out for #1 and get our essential needs met before we can be of service to anyone. And the more of our needs that are met, the greater service we may be to others. It's only when we stop our energy at the 1st Chakra that we get into trouble. We may be a little *James-Bondish* at times but most of us are not one-dimensional characters and we can both meet our needs and care for others.

GENERATING ENERGY

So, having just expounded upon the self-serving qualities

of James Bond I feel it is also important to point out here that there is actually nothing casual about sex. The power and ability to *make people* is a tremendous gift which means of course it is also a responsibility and comes with heavy consequences. And whether you conceive during sex or not, the joining of bodies via the genitals triggers a joining on multiple levels – chemical, emotional, mental, Spiritual. The word "intercourse" means the intersection of hearts (in French 'heart' = le 'cour'). When you are engaging your life force via sex you are literally throwing your entire being into the act. You are not only opening yourself up to another's entire being you are sharing your life-force with another. Talk about power, vulnerability and letting your Warrior's defenses down! There is nothing meaningless or casual about it.

Kundalini is a term from the East which represents our life-force – which symbolically originates at the base of the spine (Root Chakra) and travels upwards, enriching and animating your whole being. Sex is not the only way to raise your Kundalini but it certainly will stir up these powerful forces, and so in the light of Eastern wisdom we see that managing our sexual energy becomes even more important. The tapping and conscious channeling of this energy is the topic of other books and I encourage all to examine this subject – if not for yourself then for the friends and family members you may be of service to one day.

ASTROLOGICAL EXAMPLES

We have all come across folks in our experience who seem to share a strong affinity for the Root Chakra

– workaholics, athletes, health-nuts and those with a much higher than average libido. Other less obvious examples include doctors, massage therapists, dancers, healers of all kinds, chefs and restaurateurs, construction workers – anyone whose work centers on the body and its care and survival.

The two astrological signs ruled by Mars are Aries and Scorpio. Anyone with an Aries or Scorpio Sun, Moon or Ascendant is likely to experience their Root Chakra and the issues of survival more acutely than average. But they are not the only ones likely to feel this way. We all have a Root Chakra and we all feel it strongly from time to time. The three examples given – Sun, Moon, Ascendant – are a start to the list of astrological indicators of a strong Root. Others include those with Mars itself in the signs Aries or Scorpio, those with Mars in close aspect to their Sun, Moon or Ascendant, Mars in close aspect to their Sun's ruler or their Ascendant's ruler, those with Mars near an angle of the chart, those with Mars emphasized by placement or aspect... the list goes on. What I am getting at here is that anyone may have an active Root Chakra and emphasize those survival issues – it's not just Aries and Scorpios.

We usually know our friends and family member's birthdays so it is easier to see this pattern in the Scorpios and Aries we know. One friend I know who is a Scorpio has a child. Just the one. And while some Root Chakra people will express their survival instinct by having far more than the average number of children, this man has concentrated all his attention upon his one offspring – and the only possible chance of the survival of his genes. At least one picture of this child adorns *every* wall in the house – bedroom walls, kitchen walls, hallway walls. Desktops, dresser tops, refrigerator doors, shelves... everywhere you can put a picture. All his activities are centered around the child and the child's schedule. This is an extreme example but we all know those who place undue attention on their children as well as those on the other extreme (obviously having greater focus on other areas of life) whom we notice due to the lack of attention they pay their children. We are all a bit different in the amount of interest and inclination we have for different areas of life.

KEEPING THE ROOT CHAKRA FIT

Mind, body, spirit and emotion are all linked and when our Root Chakra is unhappy it will naturally affect all other areas of life. Luckily, this Chakra is perhaps the simplest one to support. Just getting up out of your seat, throwing your shoulders back and taking a deep breath can do wonders for your state of mind. From there, more intense movement will produce greater results. I often counsel those of my clients who are Mars-heavy to go to the gym, climb a mountain, or run around the block 20 times if they have access to neither. On a regular basis! Exerting yourself to the point of exhaustion brings about a wonderful exhilaration that also serves to calm the mind and burn off emotional energy. Food is another obvious way to support an over-taxed Root Chakra. You truly are what you eat – on both a physical and Spiritual level and nutritious food tends to be higher in energetic value, while factory farmed and factory processed foods tend to weigh us down physically, which impacts the rest of our being. Eating real food, drinking clean water, moving your body daily and sleeping nightly are key to addressing Root Chakra imbalances.

MOVING UP

So, having had our physical needs met we are now ready to engage in any sort of activity or pursuit. And our first inclination is to *do* something fun.

Chapter 2

SACRAL CHAKRA – VENUS

"… to Create…"

The 2nd chakra is where we start to have fun. Using the analogy of a child, the 1st Chakra represents the beginning – the birth or appearance on the stage of life and getting settled into a physical existence. Once we are established and our survival needs met, the first thing a child will do is *play*. We are not punching a clock just yet. We are not providing for ourselves. Our time and attention is focused on exploring the world around us and having fun doing it.

Creativity is our prime activity. The Bible introduces this notion at its very beginning. God/Spirit penetrates Matter and the result is Creation of the world. It's the very first, or primary, activity of God once he arrives on the scene. He then proceeds to "create Man in his own Image" – a marvelous clue to Human nature – for if we are made in God's image and God's first activity is creation then we too are primarily Creators. The physical example is obvious, as a quick look around you will show that the world is full of things made by people – cars, clothes, houses, etc. The role of the mind is another recently understood fact of our creative process. Films such as *The Secret* and *What The Bleep Do We Know?* have in recent years introduced us to the notion that, through our thoughts and feelings, we are actually creating our reality and our perception of reality – at all times! And this brings up another key point – these Chakras are not *on* at times and *off* at others. The flow of energy through the body is constant as long as we are alive. These forces are not optional – they are hard-wired, if you will, into our system. So creation is a non-stop process whether we are feeling particularly artistic or not.

GODDESS OF LOVE

Venus lends energy to the creative process via Passion. Venus is the goddess of passion, romance, beauty and art. We have come to distil her many facets into the title "Goddess of Love"; however 'love' is possibly the most confusing (if not the most dangerous) word in the English language. So let's distinguish between 'romantic love' (Venus) which we feel for a very small number of people in our lifetime and the Heart-Chakra type of '*Love*'- a quality of being which you may cultivate, experience and feel within yourself – and express towards anyone and anything (we will discuss Love in detail in Chapter 4).

YOU 'N' ME

Venus represents the subjective experience of "that which is attractive/beautiful to me". It requires 2 components – me and that which I am attracted to - *subject* and *object* (of affection). Beauty, we say, is in the eye of the beholder. And while there may be some universal standards of beauty, not everyone has a Van Gogh on their wall, not everyone thinks Miss America is hot and not everyone likes the Beatles (hard to imagine, but true). Beauty is a subjective phenomena and what *you* find attractive will not be exactly the same for everyone.

ROMANCE

Everyone has a slightly to largely different idea of what is fun, valuable, attractive and worthy of their creative energy. Romance is the most obvious example. You do not "fall in love" with everyone on the planet. Venus represents that form of love that we reserve for a very small percentage of the 7 billion people on the planet – the few people who actually get our romantic juices flowing, the ones we "fall in love" with – those people who, when we meet we feel like we've just walked into a fairytale and we want to settle down, make babies, and live happily ever after with.

When you fall in love it is with someone who has certain qualities that *you* find attractive. Not who your friend thinks is attractive. Not who your neighbor thinks is attractive. And hopefully not who your Mother thinks is attractive. Only you can say what it is you are looking for. (and you always know it when you find it).

PASSION

As mentioned, Passion is the fuel that powers Creativity. Why? Because we channel our creativity into those things we are passionate about. We consider Mozart to be a creative genius and while none of us knows for sure, it is hard to image Mozart being miserable when he was writing symphonies and concertos. In fact we read that he was consumed (to the point of obsession) with his love of music. (Note to parents – there are no reports of the young Mozart being scolded for not spending more time studying math or science, rather *his* unique gifts and talents were acknowledged and supported from an early age.)

Einstein was another creative genius who applied his passion to his work. He channeled his creative energy into the things he loved to do. Now I personally can't imagine creating physics equations as being fun – and few of us can. But for Einstein, this was his passion. And that's the thing – everyone's passion is different. Our passion is particular to us. There is no right or wrong when it comes to what we are passionate about – we just feel the way we do. No one would say Einstein should have spent more time playing music just as no one would criticize Mozart for not spending more time learning advanced math. As ridiculous as that sounds it is just as ridiculous for you to be expected to do something you don't like, date someone you are not attracted to or pour great amounts of your energy and time into work you despise. (Not to mention forcing your children to do some activity they despise.)

GENIUS

While genius is a term we usually reserve for special cases such as Mozart and Einstein, the fact is each of us is 'gifted' at something. There is something only you can do – due to your unique body, talents, attitude etc. In terms of writing music, Mozart and Bob Dylan are both considered to be geniuses. And the simple fact is – Mozart could *never* have written "Like A Rolling Stone". His genius was in composing symphonies and concertos. It is not a matter of Bob Dylan or Mozart being 'better' than the other. Rather, each pursued his own art, followed his own passion, and was thereby guided to his own genius. The rest of us may not ever be as famous as these two "geniuses" but the fact remains – each of us is uniquely talented at something and better than anyone else at doing. This is your genius. It always involves first following your passion because that is what your passions are there for – to guide you towards your purpose and your genius. And really, it requires first and foremost that one be one's self. Remaining true to your unique vision – born of your unique talents and perspective allows us all to be geniuses. No one can be better at being you than you!

MAKIN' BABIES

And so those things we find to be attractive – people, activities, places – are those things we are also passionate about. And that is where we choose to direct our creative energy. Mozart and Einstein show us how creativity in music or physics is a direct outgrowth of passion. Here in the 2nd Chakra our concern is enjoying life. Discovering what it is that we love to do, what really gets our juices flowing and then pouring our creative energy into it. Measuring the Chakras with our hands (as mentioned in the intro) you will locate your 2nd Chakra around the lower belly. And if you are a woman you will find your hand directly over your womb – the place where Humans are created. The womb and 2nd Chakra symbolize the creative force in us all – whether we bear children or not. Creativity takes many forms and the creation of a child in a woman's womb also serves as a metaphor for creativity of all kinds. Here, a clear definition of creativity is in order just in case you are still thinking it only applies to the fine arts, writing and acting. Creativity – in its most essential meaning – is the combination of two different things that, when joined together, produce a third thing – made up of parts of the two but not wholly one or the other – a unique entity having its own identity. Man and woman making a child is one example. Reese's Peanut Butter cups is another. Two different things – peanut butter and chocolate combined into one delicious morsel.* To expand our definition a bit further – personal creativity occurs whenever you combine two things that have not been combined before. Artists are typically considered as being 'creative', while engineers and bricklayers are not. Creativity is thought to be somehow reserved for artists who get to create for a living.

The fact is that we are all creative whether it is recognized as our profession or not. This is where the infinite quality of creativity comes in – whether you are butcher, baker, candlestick-maker or artist you are constantly having new ideas, facing new situations, meeting new people

---

*more on accidents and creativity in Chapter 6

and being presented with new challenges and applying – when needed – new solutions.

PROBLEM-SOLVING

I was having my car worked on at a shop once, and while I sat and waited for it to be ready I observed the owner of the shop handling one issue after another – phone calls, from disgruntled suppliers, customers walking in the door with concerns, mechanics coming in for consultation and instruction, delivery drivers bringing in packages. When he finally had a moment to rest I asked the owner, "How much of your job would you say is problem-solving?" His answer – 90% at least. Our success at problem-solving depends to a great deal on our willingness to entertain new ideas and apply them where needed – our ability to apply what we know in a myriad of ways to address the myriad of conditions that the world throws at us. No two people are the same and no two answers or solutions will be exactly the same every time.

LEADING THE WAY

The ability to think creatively is what sets many leaders and otherwise successful people apart from the rest. Venus is our embodied Feminine Principle (receptivity). She is open. I remember hearing an interview with John Cleese, one of the writers, actors and creative geniuses of *Monty Python's Flying Circus*. He was discussing how they would all get together and make up the next show. The key to their creativity, he said, was that they never used the word "no" when discussing ideas. *No* is not receptive. *No* is a closed door where creativity cannot enter. Rather, the conversation and ideas were allowed to swirl around the room – some ideas morphing into other ideas or sparking completely different ideas in others members of the cast which would lead to another comedic stroke of genius. But no one ever said to another, "No, that's a terrible idea". That would have been slamming the door on creativity. By leaving the door open it allowed for levels of creativity and humor never before seen.

BREAKING UP IS HARD TO DO

The *fun* that comes from having your creative juices flowing is itself one of the creations that arises when two people get together – for coffee or romance. The fun you have with this person or that person is a unique combination of your two energies and cannot be duplicated with anyone else. When we add romance to the mix – when we connect with someone who gets more of our creative juices flowing than anyone else – we find our creative powers peaking and it feels fantastic! Conversely, the arguments and fights that so often occur between ourselves and our lovers feel terrible. The creative flow is seriously restricted during an argument. What makes it even more painful is the knowledge that it has been, and could be, better than in that moment when you are fighting. And so the creative potential you share keeps you coming back for more. You may one day love another just as much or more than you love this person. But you will never love anyone else *like* you love this one. That energy – the baby – that the two of you create by being together can only be created by the two of you.

This is one reason why casual sex can leave you feeling emotionally empty. Aside from not having that person around to help navigate the emotional issues that come up around the sex-act, when your creative spark is ignited by another in a sexual encounter and then immediately doused, the sense of loss can be painful. First the physical and energetic pleasure of your creative potential being unleashed full-force is felt – and then it's gone. That sense of emptiness is the realization that this beautiful creation – this child of your creativity – did not live long, and the acute awareness of the potential that will now never be fulfilled hangs like a cloud over you.

NO TIME

In Astrology, the 5th house is representative of creativity, romance and children. Creativity was running rampant when you were a child – children actually need very little in the way of toys to be happy. Their imaginations – the spark of creative thought – are uninhibited and free to roam where they will. They create games with rocks, sticks and blades of grass if they have to. One thing about children that also applies to romance and your personal creativity – is that they are not looking at the clock. They are fully present in *the moment* – that place where time has no meaning. So too, when you are in your creative flow time no longer exists – doing something you love whether it is work or play, art or construction, lawyering or teaching or spending time with your lover.

GUIDANCE

Our passions – romantic and otherwise – are there for a purpose. Just as everyone has different creative urges, activities they enjoy and people they are attracted to, everyone has a different purpose or mission in life. Your passions are there to guide you towards your purpose.

That's why they are different for everyone. The late, great Joseph Campbell coined the term that elegantly sums up this notion – *Follow Your Bliss*. Your bliss is given to you as a guidance system. If you were told exactly what you were meant to do with this lifetime – say when you were 5 years old, there wouldn't be any mystery, there wouldn't be any exploration, there would be no learning from trial and error and there wouldn't be nearly as much fun. Rather we are given these passions, preferences and desires to help us discover our path. Boredom is the antithesis of Venus – she craves excitement, fun and passion.

THE LOVE DRUG

Venus is the one for whom the song "Addicted To Love" was written. She is forever in pursuit of that feeling of euphoria one experiences when we "fall in love". In Mythology, Venus is known as a flirt and an adulteress – she sleeps around – discovering as we all do that eventually the love drug wears off, that this person actually has some faults and annoying habits that we didn't notice before (love is blind). I don't like your cooking, you don't like my Mother, your feet stink, and so on. Venus moves from god to god – and man to man – to sustain that drug-like high. Actually, the drug analogy has a factual basis as we now know that oxytocin and other chemicals are released into the blood during states of Euphoria. So too, we may find ourselves deciding to 'move on' after the effects of falling in love have worn off – days, weeks or months after that initial hit. The love-junkie exists in all of us. We all crave that sense of oneness, inseparability and intimacy that falling in love brings – just as we crave the time spent in the creative "zone" and wish it could last forever, too. And just in case you are feeling hopeless at this point, we will be looking at the Love that transcends the ups and downs of romantic love and keeps couples together when we get to the Heart Chakra (skip ahead to chapter 4 now if you are feeling really depressed). For Venus, the high is all she can see and she spends time with those that can keep her creative juices flowing at full force.

INTERPERSONAL CREATIVITY

Speaking of couples, let's look at the energy of two. While the 1st Chakra was mostly concerned with taking care of its own needs – I, Me, Mine… the 2nd Chakra is about *us*. What can *we* create together? And how much fun can we have doing it? Let's face it – creating, doing, eating, being, dancing with another is simply more *fun* than doing these things alone. In fact, it is no fun at all to eat alone. You may enjoy your food and it may be delicious but you are not really having *fun* with your food (unless of course you are throwing it, but there again, it is infinitely more fun to throw your food at someone rather than at the wall). Creating alone is wonderful and many are called to do so and are extremely gifted at doing so. However it's not the same as creating in pairs (or groups). Fun comes from the spontaneity and mystery that comes with interacting. You don't know what that other person is about to say or do. You don't know what you will say or do next because that depends upon what the other person says or does which you won't know until it happens – and then your creative mind comes up with a response. Whether you are writing a song (Lennon/McCartney), creating a television show (Monty Python), conducting a board meeting or out on a date – the element of the unknown keeps you alert and receptive to the changing elements. It hones your creative abilities and increases the pleasures you experience by being in a body.

HELP FOR YOUR SACRAL CHAKRA

Creativity works best as a *flow* of energy. *Allowing* things to be and *acceptance* of things as they are are two attitudes that serve as energetic 'open doors' that promote flow of your creative energies. I once attended a songwriting workshop where the brilliant and successful Darryl Scott explained his process. He said when a song was 'coming through' he just wrote it down without stopping to punctuate, correct spelling or otherwise edit. And most importantly – he did not judge what was coming through. Judging – like thinking "aw, that's a stupid line" or "this is a stupid song" is the energetic equivalent of NO and slamming the door of your creativity shut. You don't really know where one line might lead to and so stopping to judge it prevents the next verse from unfolding. The *flow* is interrupted by judgment of our creative expression. Editing does have its place – specifically in the 3rd Chakra – but during the creative process it acts like a dam.

When you find yourself reflexively judging others, you know it is time to get busy with your own creative pursuits – time to get into a place where you can allow your creative juices to flow uninterrupted. And you don't have to have an 'official' creative outlet or recognized hobby. Singing in the shower when no one is home works for many. And going outdoors and playing with sticks and rocks at any age is the simplest way to prime your creative pump and get the flow back.

ASTROLOGY AND CULTURAL ARCHETYPES

Venus rules the signs Taurus and Libra. Taurus represents pure Feminine energy and Venus in her earthy Taurus expression is all about pleasure and the sensual enjoyment of life. Libra, the air-sign expression of Venus correlates to physical perfection as well as beautiful ideas such as justice, fairness and equality. The image of the blindfolded woman holding the scales of justice is a Libran image.

For the 2nd chakra I offer two archetypes – one male, one female. The first is perhaps the most beautiful woman and one of the most talented actresses in the history of American film. Exceedingly beautiful, with a most rare shade of violet/blue for her eye color, a voluptuous figure and perfect face, Elizabeth Taylor embodied the goddess as much as anyone in American culture. Passion and creativity were central to her career and love life – she could not or would not stay married to the same man for very long. Falling in love and falling out of love is a way of life for the Venusian character. Elizabeth Taylor married a total of seven men, including two marriages to Richard Burton. This particular Venusian, however, was neither Taurus or Libra. In fact she had no planets in either sign. What she did have in her chart was Venus being influenced by a number of significant planets. Just to remind you – there is so much more to your chart – especially in determining which planets/chakras are going to be strongly felt – than just Sun, Moon and Rising Sign.

Our second Archetype is the great Texas singer-songwriter

and guitar player, Taurus Willie Nelson. Exceedingly prolific as a songwriter, exceptionally unique in his vocal phrasing and immensely creative in his guitar playing. Anyone who has seen Willie perform live will attest to his out-of-the-box guitar-playing style. Those of us from Austin have a saying about Willie – "He can't play it the same way once". Willie Nelson also apparently can't stop creating children, having fathered seven to date. Both of these real people are examples of Venus operating at full force – with an unstoppable, immense creative focus, an intense attraction to love and relationship. Willie is well-known, like another famous Venusian – Libra John Lennon – to prefer to create with others. In addition to almost always performing with his family band rather than solo, Willie has also collaborated with numerous other artists – Julio Iglesias and Merle Haggard just to name two.

TOP OF THE CHARTS

And just so you don't think it's all fun and games, our 3rd Chakra gives us an additional element that each of these wonderful performers and creative geniuses cultivated and honored to help propel them into the history books.

Chapter 3

SOLAR PLEXUS CHAKRA – SATURN
"... and Establish Things..."

The 3rd Chakra is where things get serious. Saturn* –our planetary companion for the 3rd Chakra is the planet of form, structure, density, rules, discipline, mastery and the bringing into form those 'things' we chose to identify with. Just as your physical Solar Plexus is the location of your physical center of gravity, the energy of the 3rd Chakra is the densest and heaviest of the 7 – its planet, Saturn, corresponding in Alchemical lore to the element Lead. Dense. Heavy. Solid.

---

*astrologer Rick Levine points out that the symbol for Saturn – when flipped over to its mirror-image – looks much like the letters 'S' and 'T', and how almost every word in English that has 'st' in it is evocative of Saturnine energy. You will find such words throughout this chapter as well as the number 30 – also evocative of the 3rd Chakra.

Solidity as a human being tends to develop over time. One is not born as a stable, independent, self-sustaining individual – we become so as we age. The older we get, typically the more stable and productive we become. In fact, the Greek god from whom the Romans borrowed to help create their Saturn is Cronos – from where we get words such as Chronology, Chronicle and Chronometer – all related to Time.

Images such as "Father Time" and his medieval counterpart "The Grim Reaper" bring to mind this most interesting fact of life – we all have a finite amount of "time" to live our lives and yet one never knows how much one has. Those of us who grasp this fundamental fact of our existence early-on tend to be the more serious-minded, goal-oriented or ambitious amongst us – knowing that the more time they spend learning and practicing some 'thing' the better at it they will become.

The word 'establish' here denotes the making of effort, over time, towards a specific goal. The word 'manifest' is also one that fits. Manifest means to bring (a thing) into being. The word 'things' can be used interchangeable with words like 'stuff' or 'items' to signify the physical nature of our existence. Every non-naturally occurring 'thing' around us was made by another human – cars, houses, clothes, tools, roads and so on. The 3rd Chakra is where the creative spark of the 2nd Chakra takes shape. The artist has taken a creative 'idea' and 'established' it by painting, drawing or sculpting it – literally putting into physical form.

Sometimes we may have a brilliant idea that we do not establish in the physical. As creative beings who are creating constantly, it may be impossible to manifest every single creative idea that comes to us. But there are some ideas that – feeling most passionate about – we choose to dedicate ourselves, our time and energy to and actually bring into 'being'.

The word 'things' here not only represents actual physical stuff – that which you can touch, taste, see, smell or hear – it also stands for those 'things' which are not technically physical and yet are a part of your physical experience, and will not be a part of your experience after you have left this body. Attitude, lifestyle, career and some aspects of our personality are all examples of things that we create and establish that shape our identity while here on earth. They are very real in our physical experience, yet we don't imagine them to be a part of the afterlife.

GROWING UP

Though we are born with the essence of our personality, our self-identity is shaped over time. As we grow and learn about the physical world and experience different ideas, people and events, we begin to form our own ideas about life and our role within the larger picture. When we are young we rely upon others to show us the ropes – how to dress, how to use a fork and knife, how to tie our shoes. When we start school we are shown how to read, write, do math. As we grow into older and older children we are taught right from wrong. Parents, teachers and preachers are all tasked with showing us how to get along in our culture. We are taught to obey the laws and rules and shown how if we fail to obey there are consequences – such as being grounded, having privileges taken away and going to jail. As a child – or in other words, as a non-individuated, non-responsible person – you are surrounded (and hopefully supported) by external authority figures – those who know more than you do about living in the physical world in general and your culture in particular, and who guide and instruct you so that you may successfully integrate into them.

The apprentice and disciple are examples of those who have intentionally entered into a relationship of learner to teacher or Master. Here, discipline evolves from an externally imposed form of harsh rules and regulations to a voluntarily entered into condition where one has chosen to dedicate one's time and energy to learning a craft – how to become a certain 'thing' such as butcher, baker, candlestick-maker, etc.

The transition from child to adult involves the distilling of the pure creative spark of 2nd Chakra energy into a useful, productive, tangible form – a career and a personality with values, things you cherish, things you believe in, things you don't believe in, things that "matter" to you. When one has a clear sense of self, one becomes personally powerful. Becoming imbued with a sense of what really matters leads one to take a stand. Standing in a particular place, saying "this is who I am, this is what I believe in, this is what I am all about" is to consolidate your energy into a very focused and strong presence. The 3rd Chakra therefore represents *power* – that is to say, *personal power*. The power that comes from knowing what you want to be in life and taking the needed steps to become that. The person who knows exactly what they like and don't like, what they believe in and what they are willing to take a stand for, has intestinal fortitude and a strength of character that help propel them more forcefully towards their goals. Size and age do not matter. Although children typically do not become so focused until older, we have all met certain kids who have much figured out about life – seemingly ahead of schedule. Just as we have met adults – some in to their 40s, 50s or 60s! – who are still struggling to find an anchor in this life.

The Solar Plexus Chakra is what holds you in one place, around which the rest of the physical universe may revolve, aggregate and be formed (and informed) by your presence. The power inherent in a person who is well-integrated, focused and willing to take a stand for what they believe in is as strong as any force known to humanity. History is replete with examples of men and women who have literally changed the course of history through the force of their own will and the loyalty and admiration it evokes in those around them.

POWER

The 3rd Chakra is then considered our Power Center. And here, power should be understood to mean physical or material power. Spiritual power is focused and expressed differently and we will discuss this at length in the following chapters. But here in the 3rd we are chiefly concerned with successfully navigating the physical world. Here, the creative, passionate spark of Venus becomes tempered in the fires of Time. Just as pressure over time transforms the lump of coal into the diamond, the pressures of growing up, the pressures to break out of the carefree, Venusian attitude of pure creativity and choose one passion to cultivate, present themselves as we enter into our 20s. Those with a clear sense of self tend to get on track earlier. The Beatles who symbolically conquered the world in their mid-twenties are an example. Others may spend their 20s studying, changing their course of study at school, trying different jobs to see what they like, spending time travelling to get a better sense of the world, and thereby their own place within it. As we approach age 30 – if we haven't already – we tend to buckle-down and get serious about life. For some it can be a time of existential crises as we struggle to cling to the carefree days of our Venusian youth while the increasing responsibilities of life demand we become more stable. The question put to us when we were children – "What do you want to be when you grow up?" now insists on being answered.

SATURN RETURN

In astrology, the Saturn Return is the phenomenon of reaching this existential crisis just as the planet Saturn is returning to the same degree of the Zodiac it was occupying when you were born. It takes Saturn 29½ to 30 years or so to make a complete revolution around the Sun. It is at this point in our lives when we start to feel the need to settle into some 'thing' that will define us and sustain us through the rest of our lives (again, a consideration of time). The youth of our first 30 years gives way to that stage of life known as our "prime of life". Having experimented, learned, perhaps taken time to travel and experience a range of activities and ideas, we now tend to settle in to a more clearly defined lifestyle and become focused on productivity.

Teenagers generally consider themselves to be immortal, however by our late 20s we have accumulated at least a few scars and the reality of physical limitation starts to sink in. Sometimes the existential crisis can provoke a career change. If one has seemingly "figured things out" in their 20s, they may wake up one day and have a complete reversal of direction as new values and thoughts begin to take hold. John Lennon, with his Saturn-ruled Aquarius Moon was seemingly at the top of the world when he experienced his Saturn return in 1969 and promptly quit the Beatles to embark upon his next phase of life. So the crisis need not be a physically traumatic one where life and limb are at stake. Oftentimes the crisis is one of consciousness or realization – confined to our own sense of awareness, but no less potent and certainly requiring just as much intestinal fortitude and decisiveness as a physical crisis.

THE GENIE IN THE BOTTLE

If you've seen the film "The Secret" you may recall the scene where the kid finds the Genie bottle. When you rub a Genie bottle the Genie appears and says, "Your wish is my command." This story is a metaphor for the process of taking a stand in your 3rd Chakra power center and thereby knowing what you want and then asking for it. The Universe, God or the Genie, if you prefer, is there to support and assist you in your ambitions. The trick is to be very specific about what you want. We've all heard the expression "be careful what you ask for – you may get it." When we have a clear sense of self and purpose we are in a better condition for knowing what we want and then articulating it. It's as if your center of gravity is magnetically pulling people, experiences and resources towards you – just as the Sun (Sol)* in the center of our solar system is the center of gravity and pulls planets, comets and other physical things towards it. And so the clearer you are – the more defined and focused your intentions and purpose, lifestyle, career, passion – the easier it is for the Universe to provide. If "your wish is the Universe's command" then you want to be very precise about what you command the Universe to do for you.

THE REAL WORLD

As a young man I was in the business world and I would often attend a weekly networking lunch where we would get to know one another and our businesses and then be better able to refer new clients and customer to each other. Essential to the process was our introduction – delivered at the start of lunch where we would each get 30 seconds to say our name, describe our business, and say what would be the best referral for us. 30 seconds is a very short time and so we were forced to be very precise and specific about what we wanted. The time limit was also in place to keep all of our heads from exploding with too much information. While we may all be infinite beings on the spiritual level, down here on the planet, in the body, we have a finite attention span and are simply not able or even interested in retaining everything everyone has to say at a networking lunch. So 30 seconds (have you noticed how often the number 3 is coming up in

---

*"Solar Plexus" in science denotes a *physical* center of gravity – thus the Solar Plexus Chakra is located at your physical center. The Sun will be seen in chapter 4 as the *energetic* center of gravity.

this chapter?) was just enough time to get your *essence* across – the essentials. The best at this Saturnian exercise was my friend Paul. First off, he was there every week and so we got to know him over time. At his turn each week he would stand and say something along the lines of, 'Hello, my name is Paul. I am an investment advisor. I help people plan for the future and the best referral for me is someone from age 25-35 who wants to get started saving up for their retirement now." Boom! That was it. Didn't even need the whole 30 seconds. Precise, concise, defined, focused. No one had any doubt as to what he was about and whether we knew anyone who fit his description of the kind of client he was looking for.

The opposite extreme was demonstrated by someone (whose name I do not recall, not surprisingly) who only came to lunch one time and when her turn was up she stood and said, "I'm a realtor and the best referral for me is everyone, because everyone needs a home!" at which point my eyes glazed over and my mind went completely blank. I do not know 'everyone'. I know individual people, with specific names, faces and needs. Again, our finite mind cannot focus upon and grasp every*thing* or every*one* at once and so to function effectively in the finite realm of physical matter it helps to zero in on one thing at a *time*. "Everyone" in this instance translated into "no one". Just imagine a realtor asking the Genie for "everyone" and then getting it – she'd never have time to sleep or take a day off!

NOT ENOUGH TIME

When we are children we don't usually have a clear sense of time. Psychologists tell us that as babes and young children there is no past or future – only now; at least in our perception. As we age and start to learn about time we eventually come to the realization that we don't have enough of it to do every*thing* we want. In order to become effective or proficient at some 'thing' we must dedicate more time to it. Practice and self-discipline become our allies as we first choose an occupation (something to occupy ourselves with) and then start *doing* it. And the longer we do it the better at it we become – Mastery as a result of discipline or discipleship. "Practice makes perfect" is a common saying. I would add that practice makes you *what* you are. A doctor is said to practice medicine, a lawyer to practice law. A violin player is only so because he or she picks up the violin and plays it – almost every day of their life. Practice is something you do over *time* and if you do not practice what you call your art or profession then you are not really that. What we choose to do over time has a way of defining us.

THE CLOCK

Time pieces have also received a bad rap over the years. "Punching the clock" is analogous to having a dead-end job that you hate. The tolling of a church bell can signify the calling of 'the faithful to their knees' as well as marking the death of a church member.[4] And many of us have at one time or another been a slave to the alarm clock. But if you want to get something done, if you want to achieve something, the clock can be your best friend. The (material) world is run by those who show up, and if you are going to create something powerful and productive, you will often need other people's help. And you need them to all show up at the same time. The clock is the servant of the *boss*. If you are 'working for the Man' just to 'pay the bills' it's no wonder you dread the alarm going off in the morning. If you are dedicating your life to a purpose – whether you are employee or employer – the clock becomes *your* servant.

HIPPIES AND THE ESTABLISHMENT

Let's go back to the 2nd Chakra for a moment so as to better understand the evolution from 2nd to 3rd. The Hippies of the 1960s are the embodiment of 2nd Chakra/Venusian energy. Sex. Drugs. Rock'n'Roll. Fun, Fun, Fun. Free love. Flower Power. Hippies represented 2nd Chakra energy in its full-on, heightened expression. Even the word "hippie" denotes one who operates from their 2nd Chakra – that area of the body between one's *hips*. And of course the mantra of those freedom-loving, anti-establishment youth was "Don't trust anyone over 30". Because over 30 – that post-Saturn Return phase of life – was when your creative energy supposedly stopped flowing free and became solidified and stagnant – trapped and imprisoned in a boring, straight, dead-end reality with – god forbid – responsibilities! Going to work for "the Man". Selling your soul to fit into "the Establishment". Of course the establishment was completely corrupt and the hippies had good reason not to trust it.

However, a funny thing happened on the way to Nirvana – most of those hippies grew up, reaching 30 years of age and beyond. And free love often led to expensive children. Now with families, jobs and careers, many Hippies *became* the Establishment. And with any luck they – and you 50 years later in the 21st Century – were/are able to channel their creative energies into an occupation of their choosing. The 3rd Chakra serves to house, shape and form the 2nd Chakra's creative energy and passion – not to negate or squash it. In addition to their creative prowess, all those musicians who inspired the Hippies and the rest of the 60s culture had one thing in common – they all took the *time* to learn an instrument, practice it and not only create songs, but retain, record and perform them – manifesting their creativity into tangible, physical products that could be shared over and over and over again.

ASTROLOGICAL EXAMPLES

Capricorn and Aquarius are the two astrological signs ruled by Saturn. Typically these are the folks mentioned at the start of this chapter who have gotten a handle on life a bit earlier than most. Business owners are an example of those with a serious dose of Saturn in their charts. These are the people who can "hold it together" better than most. Boss is the perfect title for Capricorns, who have an intrinsic need to build, oversee and maintain some*thing* productive. Even as young children many Capricorns will exhibit a desire to tell their friends or other siblings what to do. I always tell parents of Capricorn children that they must be given *something* to be in charge of – even if it is a small thing. Otherwise their natural inclination will be frustrated and could result in acting out through inappropriate instances of bossiness – such as telling the parents what to do.

Judges, senators and church leaders – those upholders

of the establishment – also tend to have a strong dash of Saturn in their energetic makeup. Ironically, the Capricornian establishment's greatest challenge comes from Aquarius – the sign they share Saturn's energy with. The paradox is resolved in this way – while Capricorn's job is to *uphold* the status quo, Aquarius job is to *destroy* the status quo and then *re-establish* a new status quo. Aquarius are the mutation of the species. Those who recognize that time doesn't stand still; that life, the weather, trends, conditions and energies are constantly changing and that to remain stuck in an old paradigm in the midst of a changing Universe is to be left behind and invite stagnation and death.

THE BEAUTY OF RESTRICTION

Your 3rd Chakra is like a glass that holds water. In order to take a drink yourself or share that drink with another you must contain the water first. Even when drinking from a stream one cups his or her hand to first contain before bringing water to mouth. Saturn and the 3rd Chakra symbolize the container for your spirit so that you may effectively deliver your Spiritual essence into the physical world. Just like the river that runs from the mountain to the sea – delivering energy and matter from above – a river is defined and made possible by the banks which contain it.

The limitation and restriction represented by Saturn is the main reason he has gotten so much bad press over the centuries. No child likes to be told they "can't have this" or "can't do that" and so to the child-like mind, limitation is associated with the stifling effects of having an overbearing, external authority figure. However, a simple look in the mirror will show the great value of limitation, as we notice our bodies are contained within our skin. Without it and the support of our structural components – bones (said to be ruled by Saturn in classic astrology) – we would not be able to stand nor would we be nearly as well protected from harmful, external forces such as weather, UV rays and bacteria. The skin also helps with establishing our identity – everything inside my skin is *me*, everything outside my skin is *other*. I am here and you are there. It is a very clear, physically discernible border. So too, our energetic 3rd Chakra serves to separate and identify us by limiting our expression to the things that are most important and valuable (Venus) to us. If you choose to go to massage school you cannot go to law school – at least not at the same time. You are limited by the amount of time you have and the choices you make with that time in order that you may channel your energies into strong and personally meaningful expressions.

DOING IT WITH STYLE

One of the unforeseen products of limitation is style. Musicians and singers for example are limited by their choice of instrument, the types of music they perform, the flexibility, length and strength of their fingers, arms, vocal chords and lungs, their mental grasp of the music they play and so on. The multitude of genres of music, as well as styles of playing particular instruments and styles of singing are evidence of the *limitless* number of unique combinations of these limiting factors. Django Rhinehart – the guitarist credited by many with inventing the Gypsy swing guitar sound of the 1930s in Paris

– had the use of only 2 fingers on his left hand. And so a new style of playing was created – not out of experimentation so much as out of a necessity (the mother of invention), born of limitation.

OLD AGE HAS ITS BENEFITS

For better or worse, adults in our culture tend to give little or no credence to the words, thoughts and ideas of youngsters. This has to do with the need to live and experience your knowledge – testing and tempering it with worldly experience before it may be considered valuable "wisdom". I often tell my younger students that they are in fact geniuses that have important new contributions to make to the human dialog. However, until they have a bit of time under their belts – say about 30 years worth – they may not have had enough experience to shape their ideas into practical forms. They may also have a very limited audience amongst the older generation – those Saturnine power brokers who are (seemingly) in control of the physical world. So age does come with benefits. The longer we live the more opportunity we have to experience life and learn more about it. The disciple becomes the Master over time. Younger people have come into this world with a fresh update to the cultural program. And as brilliant as their ideas may be, the successful application of those ideas usually takes an understanding of the environment into which they are applied – an understanding which takes about 30 years or so to achieve. The biblical story of the boy Jesus is a telling example. When at age 12 he is found in the temple offering his teaching and wisdom we are told how flabbergasted everyone was. Incredible! Amazing! Fantastic! And then we don't hear another word about Jesus for 18 years! What happened to amazing and fantastic? Apparently the world was just not ready to accept brilliant and life-changing wisdom from a 12 year old. And so Jesus begins his own discipleship, gaining experience and practice until he (and the world) are ready for his formal ministry which he begins at age 30.

GETTING YOUR SATURN ON

An immediate and clear response to the question "What do you do for a living?" is one mark of a strong 3rd Chakra. Hesitation in your answer, stammering and using words such as "kinda" and "trying" are all signs that you are still unfocused. One of the beautiful things about our current Western world is that we are relatively free to choose our occupation or career, so even if you are young and not sure that you will be doing what you are doing now for the rest of your life (in fact no one really knows for sure what they will be doing next year, let alone for the rest of their life) you are free to change at any time. But at any particular moment in time – to be able to say clearly "this is what I am doing" is to have a strength and force of character that the Universe, the Genie in the bottle, your peers and even older folks will recognize and respect.

CULTURAL ARCHETYPE

Our symbolic representation of the ultimate Saturnine authority figure is the main character of the Old Testament of the Bible, Moses. As God's agent, Moses was tasked with leading and administering God's cho-sen people – the "Children of Israel". As metaphorical 'children' they were culturally and symbolically stuck in the lower Chakras – not able to tell right from wrong, requiring a 3rd Chakra, external authority figure to keep them in line. Enter the Ten Commandments. Ten rules to live by. They were not requests or suggestions and certainly not agreements. They were absolute, cut and dried verbatim commandments of God – whose Holy Day is Saturn's day (Saturday). "I am telling you what to do and how to live. No discussion necessary. Just memorize these ten rules and do what they say." How many times have we heard a parent say in response to the question "Why?" from their child "Because I said so!"? These "children" of Israel were even worshipping a golden calf or bull – the bull of course being the astrological symbol for the sign Taurus – astrologically ruled by our 2nd Chakra planet, Venus. And the length of their sojourn through the desert before reaching the Promised Land was 40 years – another number associated with Venus as the planet's 5 retrograde stations over an 8 year period (5x8=40) trace a 5-pointed star or pentagram (a symbol for witches and other feminine wisdom traditions) around the Zodiac. Additionally the gestation period of a human fetus in mother's womb (2nd Chakra) is 40 weeks.

So we see the Children (or perhaps they were the Hippies?) of Israel embarked upon a Venusian Odyssey as they struggle to evolve or raise their consciousness to the next level. In fact, most of the Old Testament is the story of children disappointing their father and being punished for disobedience. The New Testament brings us a new character who introduces us to a new way of being and an energetic evolution from the lower, physically-oriented energy centers, best described as operating from a higher level – the level of the Heart Chakra.

Chapter 4

HEART CHAKRA – THE SUN

"… that Encourage Love…"

The Heart represents the halfway point in our discussion – the center of the Chakra system. Just as the Heart Chakra occupies the center of our energetic system, so too its planetary companion – the Sun – occupies the center of our Solar System. The Heart Chakra represents the place where Spirit and Matter meet as well as the unification of opposites on the material plane. Here – distinct from Venusian/2nd Chakra love of particular objects or people, we are introduced to the notion of 'Love' as something we are capable of experiencing, feeling, showing and giving – regardless of whether we are being 'loved' back. The Heart requires no external validation to *feel* Love.

THE BRIDGE

The Heart, amongst other things, represents the bridge between Spirit and Matter – the place where the upper Chakras connect with the lower. This is a most important metaphor – for without a bridge the lower 3 Chakras symbolically remain stuck in the physical realm and the upper 3 remain stuck in the Spiritual – ungrounded and ineffective in terms of practical application into a physical world. As the bridge, the Heart belongs neither wholly in the Spiritual or the material realm but uniquely in equal parts of both. Here, pure physical energy finds Spiritual meaning and direction to guide its application. And Spiritual truths find a place to express.

HEART CHAKRA LOVE

Love is perhaps the most confusing word in the English language, so let's take a moment to define Love in the context of the Heart Chakra. Whereas Venus/Sacral Chakra is very particular about whom she loves, the Heart represents the Love that is able to be felt for anyone and everyone. As opposed to Venus and the object of her affections, the Love of the Heart is rather a condition or an aptitude that is either consciously present within your heart or not. It is an ability or skill that is exercised in the presence of external objects and in its being directed towards external objects (people) but is not dependent on those objects looking or behaving a certain way or even loving you in return.

Another interesting property of Love is that it is not a physical 'thing'. It certainly has application in the physical world but it cannot be actually seen with the physical eyes or measured in a lab. And yet it exists as the most powerful personal force known to anyone. Thus the word 'encourage' is used in our sentence. Love is not a 'thing' to be *made*. Nor can you *make* someone love (you). What you can do is 'encourage' love by the way you speak and act towards others. The French word for heart is "le cour", and so to *en-cour-age* someone is to *en-hearten* or to *put heart in* to someone. Love can be cultivated, fostered, forgotten or neglected. But as energy (remember, any 'thing' that is not a *physical* thing is energy) Love cannot be made or destroyed.

FEELINGS AND EMOTIONS

We often use these two words – feelings and emotions – interchangeably and yet there is an important distinction. Peace activist and Spiritual teacher Rennie Davis puts it this way – "emotions are chemical, feelings are electrical". That is to say, the nature of emotions is literally and figuratively the same as our experience of a chemical rush such as that of adrenaline or sugar. This definition echos Eckhart Tolle's definition of emotion as a thought with a corresponding physical response.[5] If, say, you are confronted with a mad dog, fear is the emotion that will be felt, adrenaline is the chemical that will be released into your blood stream, the fight or flight response will be triggered, your internal Root Chakra warrior is activated and you take the action needed to take care of yourself. Once you have successfully fought or fled and you are out of danger, the adrenaline stops being released into your bloodstream, you calm down, and then feel exhausted – the adrenaline crash. You may also experience a similar phenomenon with other emotions – excitement, lust,

ɼ..., other activities – exercise, competition, sex...
ɔther chemicals – sugar, drugs and alcohol.

Feelings, on the other hand, operate differently. Gratitude, for example, does not trigger adrenaline, nor does it require sugar, alcohol or any other chemical to be felt. It simply arises from your Heart when you experience or choose to dwell upon some past or present act of kindness or when you are/were receiving a gift. And while gratitude activates your Heart and you feel the effects, it doesn't wear you out to do so. There is no crash – no need to recover after a feeling is felt. Respect, compassion, kindness, appreciation do not cost you anything to feel. They are freely given gifts* – to both yourself and the receiver of your feeling.

So – gratitude, appreciation, respect, etc. – these different feelings are what I call the different colors on the love pallet – different forms or expressions of Love. And they are electrical in nature rather than chemical in that they generate energy that can be shared and transferred to others – just as an electrical current can run from one light bulb to the next on a string of lights. Rather than draining you or causing you to need to rest and recover from their expression, feelings have a way of increasing your energy as well as the energy of those around you. Joy and Love are infectious just as inspiration and encouragement are indeed passed like a current from one person to another. Another excellent metaphor is that of a candle being able to light multiple other candles without losing

---

*The word 'gift' has 4 letters. With higher numbers/chakras we will begin to see more of this numerical connection between the number of letters in certain words and the Chakras they evoke.

its own flame. The first candle may run out of wax and wick – just as our physical bodies run out of time and energy – but the flame can continue on everlasting, just as flames of inspiration have been passed along across centuries and generations by such famous lovers as Jesus and Martin Luther King, Jr.

Let us be careful not to assume that feeling is inherently superior to emotion. Emotions are an integral part of human experience and self-expression. Rather, the point to be made is that when you are operating from your Heart (your center) and you are steeped in feelings of loving kindness, the emotions that arise will be tempered by the feelings of love, and they and the resulting behavior will reflect accordingly. On the other hand, if one is ruled by their emotions, the heart symbolically takes a back seat and the emotions (positive or negative) are left to drive, which usually leads to trouble. The Spanish word for Sunday is Domingo. We are all in better shape when the Heart Chakra/Sun is dominating our lives.

Emotions then, can best be seen as tools to be guided by the Heart rather than as central, dominating forces. When your Heart is guiding you, the emotions then become fuel to power the delivery of your core feelings – amplifying your vibration if you like – just as your physical heart-rate will increase with emotion, so too the energetic impact of your Heart Chakra increases at the same time.

SCIENCE AND THE HEART

Research has shown that the human Heart works best when it is feeling Love. With modern technology, scientists are able to measure such things as the heart's strength, stability and numerous other factors. These factors all improve when we are feeling gratitude, compassion, joy, love, etc. Not surprisingly, the strength of our hearts as measured by these same factors will *decrease* when we feel anger, hatred and fear. These scientific findings show us a few very important things. First, we function better when we are loving. Second, we function worse when we are experiencing emotions such as hatred and fear. And if we function better when loving and worse when we are feeling the opposite, it shows us that we are in fact made to Love. This is the feeling state that allows us to be our best, to operate more fully. A loving Heart serves us and a hateful, angry heart literally hurts us. We have all recognized the power of Love in our own being and in the lives of others. Now science shows us a companion physical benefit to living with a Spiritual orientation – another example of the meeting of spirit and matter within the Heart. We are made to Love. This is why our Hearts work better physically when we are doing so. We function best when we are Loving. *Purpose* – as mentioned in the intro – is a direct outgrowth of *function*. If for example, I have feathers and wings not only do I fly but I am *made* to fly. It is an essential feature of my purpose. Fish are made to swim. Our hearts function best when we are Loving. That is what *they* are made to do. The heart represents that place where our physical well-being is directly tied to our energetic/feeling/Spiritual well being – the meeting or bridge between our physical reality and our Spiritual nature.

GIVING LOVE

Just as the Sun is constantly giving light and warmth to the Solar System, the Heart – as long as you are alive – is constantly beating and sending blood to the body. The energetic parallel is that as long as your heart is beating you are also sending the energy of your feelings out into the world that surrounds you. When you are feeling love, everyone around you feels it, too. The same with anger. And powerful feelings coupled with powerful emotions send out powerful energy. We have all had the experience of being around someone who is so full of love – a recently married or newly parented person comes to mind – that we are affected by their joy. *We* begin to feel more uplifted and joyful by sharing in another's joy. Other's fear and anger will also affect us. Have you ever been creeped-out or scared by someone in the room or someone on the bus who is about to burst with anger? Good or bad, our feelings and emotions are being shared with those around us. We are giving energy to the planet and the whole human family – all the time! As long as we live. It is what we do – therefore we are *purposed* to do so. Just as the Sun must shine and the heart must beat – you must and are sharing your energy with those around you.

The astrological sign Leo (the King), its ruler the Sun, and the Heart Chakra in this sense are primarily masculine* in their nature – love is to be given first and foremost. It is best expressed by action – something you do. In other words you perform acts that are inspired by feelings of love. There is of course the feminine and receptive aspect

---

*at their most fundamental level, masculine=giving, feminine=receiving

of Love and the Heart as well – just as there are two chambers of the heart that receive blood and two that send blood. In fact the two modes are complementary and make each other possible – just as all factors in our dualistic world are tied to their opposite factors. However the receiving part of love requires that Love be given first and tends to be easier for most whereas the giving of Love seems to be more scarce. The Sun and Mars represent our two main masculine centers (just as the Moon and Venus represent the two main feminine centers). If too much of your masculine energy is tied up in 1st Chakra activity – f**ing, fighting and surviving – the Heart suffers from a lack of support and finds it has little energy available to it for generating love. As a masculine function – doing, projecting, delivering – it requires energy. The fact that our world is constantly engaged in a state of warfare – from the personal level to the global is a demonstration of one of the things that happens to a culture whose Heart is drained by an over-stimulated Mars/Root Chakra.

THE ART OF LOVING

Erich Fromm, in his book "The Art of Loving" describes the active function of love by saying "love is a verb".[6] It requires activity or enactment in order to be valid. In other words – here at the bridge between spirit and matter, the feeling component alone makes less impact in the physical world if it is not coupled with physical expression – *acts* of kindness, care and respect. The Bible refers to this when discussing "Faith without Works". The two are linked and to have one without the other is a cheat or a half-measure; leaving the experience of both the giver and the receiver feeling incomplete. This actually touches upon one of the major themes of this book and the philosophy behind it – the fact that we are a combination of spirit and matter and as such we are designed to blend both elements into everything we do – work, play, thoughts, actions, feelings, etc. Nowhere is this more apparently symbolic than in the Heart. The Heart symbolizes the blender where all opposites are combined to create that which can only be created when the two are brought together. The position of the hands during prayer is a direct portrayal of the this metaphor – the left hand and the right hand, yin and yang, feminine and masculine, meet at the heart – the blender, the bridge – the place where opposites meet, where dualistic matter is brought into an awareness of Unity – the defining characteristic of spirit.

PARADOX OF THE HEART

So far we have identified love as a *feeling* (spirit) and a *verb* (matter). It is an ability of ours and motivates us to perform actions that are not dependent upon another's response. Liberated from the dependency upon an object we experience with Venus, the Love of the Heart/Sun is free to operate at any time, under any circumstance and be directed towards anyone. And this is the interesting thing – as here in the Heart we are in a sort of twilight zone where the rules of physics and custom are somewhat warped. Your ability to love is your own – it is singular and complete, and at the same time, in order for it to be real – in order for it to *matter* – it must be expressed in the physical world or given to another – and so we seem to have the subject/object dynamic again. The trick is the blending of the singular ability to love with the subject/

object experience and not confusing your ability to love (the Sun) with the Venusian expectation of reciprocation – which usually runs along the lines of "If I love you, I expect you to love me back". When we re-consider Love to be a gift, freely given, we can avoid the temptation to *adulterate* our Love or *bring it down* into a narcissistic and material experience that requires external validation.

THE WORD IS LOVE

Love – without qualification – stands on its own; sovereign and self-sustaining, because it is an expression of that which is divine or outside of the dualistic, physical realm. If I were to define Love it would be this:

As humans, we have and need a word for every thing so that we may communicate our ideas effectively. So when we see kindness, compassion, care, respect, gratitude, appreciation, joy, awe, etc. in the words and actions of ourselves and others – the activities inspired by these Spiritually-sourced feelings – we use the word "Love". *Love is the recognition of the presence of Spirit operating in the physical world.*

As a powerful, divine, endless force, Love needs no qualifiers. This is why phrases such as "pure love" and "unconditional love" are actually disempowering. Once you qualify a Spiritual power with a word such as "unconditional", you have symbolically *dragged it down* into a lower (physical) level where it and its opposite now exist side by side. This may seem like a minor, semantic point but it's extremely important! If you can have "unconditional" love then you can and must have "conditional love" And of course there is no such thing as conditional love because Love is without condition. Therefore there is no such *thing* as unconditional love. The word 'unconditional' is itself a condition. It is accurate to say love is without condition but to speak the phrase 'unconditional love' is entirely different and energetically weakening that which is the strongest force in the world. As the strongest force there is, Love really needs no help from lesser words.* To qualify it with words like "unconditional" is to adulterate – to make impure – that which is pure, to drag a Spiritual reality into the realm of duality without its Spiritual nature intact. Love is one of those very rare and special *things* that are not things – best expressed without qualifiers or adjectives. It is a non-material feeling that exists in the Hearts of people. It is Spiritual presence in a physical world. It defies scientific measurement and physical observation and at the same time exists as the most powerful force known on this planet.

LEO – THE KING

King, along with *gift* is another 4-letter word that embodies the energy of the Sun and the Heart Chakra. Kings are mostly a thing of the past and so a brief definition is in order. The King in ancient times was understood to be God's (or the gods') representative on Earth – the literal, physical presence of the Spiritual force. As such the King was the channel through which that energy flowed into the people – thus the idea of the King/Heart being a giver, a masculine *expression* of energy.

Leo is the one astrological sign ruled by the Sun. So far you may have noticed that each planet rules two signs.

---

*more on the power of words in Chapter 5

The Sun and the Moon are different of course and as such they are awarded special status in the astrological hierarchy – ruling one sign each. The traditional King is the bestower of gifts and the King's court (from the French "le cour"), the center of the Kingdom. Thus we see the incessant giving that is the hallmark of so many of our Leo friends as well as a need to command the center of attention. This need to be in the center is not necessarily as negative as it may seem at first. As a "Sun/Son of God", those with Solar emphasis in their charts, such as Leos, identify strongly with the notion of being here explicitly to deliver God's bounty to the rest of us. When Leo is at the center she/he is equally accessible to everyone.

ARCHETYPE OF THE HEART

Our primary archetype – Jesus – the 'Son/Sun of God', is an example of one who bridged the physical and Spiritual worlds and achieved a perfected state of being – where the physical actions are enlightened by Spiritual awareness. The words of Jesus that come to us through the Gospels are chocked-full of solar analogy and metaphor.

It is important to recall that Jesus was a Jew preaching to other Jews. His statement "the law is written in your heart" is reference to the Law of Moses – our 3rd Chakra archetype. Jesus here is describing an evolution from Solar-Plexus Chakra consciousness to Heart Chakra consciousness. The idea is that – as the heart serves as the symbolic bridge between spirit and matter, if your consciousness is stopped or stuck at the 3rd Chakra level it does not have access to Spiritual energy and information – thus the need for an external authority figure who does have access to spirit (Moses). Elevating your consciousness to your Heart Chakra is the way you become *self*-aware; you are now in direct contact with Spiritual truth and no longer need an external authority figure to tell you what to do. Thus the Law – the Spiritual truths and guidelines essential for living on this planet – are now available to you when you have raised your consciousness to the level of your Heart. In other words, you have now grown from a Child of God into an Adult of God – once you have raised your consciousness above the purely physical plane and are operating with Heart consciousness – where Spiritual truths and physical actions are combined.

One of the most powerful teachings Jesus made is also the one that is least remembered. I read a very interesting book when I was in my twenties called "The 100: A Ranking of the Most Influential Persons in History".[7] Jesus came in at number three! Of course I was shocked as a member of a Christian culture to find that my #1 was only third best in the world. The author explained however, the reason why Muhammad came in at number one and Jesus a bit further down the list, 1) because there were many, many more Muslims in the world than Christians and 2) and most importantly – as Jesus was a Jewish rabbi, coming from a long line of rabbis preaching Jewish Doctrine to Jewish people – most of what he said had already been said before him. And the one exception, the one truly original teaching of Jesus, according to the author, was the teaching to "love your enemy" which as it turns out no one remembers and almost no one practices.

Love your enemy changes the entire ball game! Instead

of the Venusian concept of loving those who love you back – friends, family, members of your tribe or culture, and hating those who are opposed to you – your personal enemies, belligerent States, other races, other religions – loving your enemy requires you to operate from a different level with a different understanding of what Love is. "The Sun shines on your enemy as well as your friend" said Jesus. Hating your enemy, as science has shown us, causes one to weaken one's self. Now I'm not suggesting that you not defend yourself when being attacked. However you may defend yourself without hating that person who is attacking. I recall hearing a story from a martial artist who was engaged in competition with a formidable opponent. He was seemingly outmatched but at one point in the match he was able to sense anger coming from his opponent at which point he knew he would win because, not only was his opponent weakening himself, he was also operating in a predictable manner – providing a chink in his armor, so to speak, which could be exploited. Loving our enemies rather than hating them also helps diffuse a tense situation – especially when we are, let's say, in an argument with a spouse or friend. To respond to anger with patience or love or kindness rather than reactively responding in kind can prevent the escalation of harsh emotion and help calm an angry person in many cases. Loving our enemy is not just religious dogma, it is a practical way of moving through the world.

SUN OF GOD

In the Christian Mythos, Jesus is a solar deity – giving love, preaching love, embodying love, born on the day the Sun has risen one degree above its lowest point in the sky – December 25th – as are all the other "sons of god" in the other religions, symbolizing the return or the Victory of the Sun. The story of Jesus' crucifixion and resurrection are also symbolic of the evolution of consciousness up to the Heart/4th Chakra. Jesus' crucifixion and death occur on Friday (Viernes in Spanish) or Venus Day. He is then said to have gone to Hell to wrestle with the Devil on Saturday (Saturn's/Satan's day). Then and only then is he resurrected on *Sun*-day. This metaphor symbolizes the replacing of Venus and the emotions as the dominant center of one's being with the Sun and feelings of love. Venus is a goddess – a *personified* symbol with strengths *and* weaknesses. The Sun simply is. There is no god or goddess who entirely embodies the Sun (or Moon). The Jews of Jesus' and Moses' time were (like most cultures/nations/peoples) extremely Venusian. You are either one of us (Jews) or not (Gentiles). We are God's chosen people and you are not. God is on our side, not yours. Just like our internal Venus – romantically loving this guy but not that guy – the god of the Jews played favorites. The resurrection story symbolizes the triumph of the Heart over this 2nd Chakra (Friday) world-view as well as a bypassing of the 3rd Chakra (Saturn's day) need for external authority figures, to establish the Heart as the conceptual center of one's life. Jesus' descent from the Jewish "King David" and his title "King of the Jews" are also telling clues.

SUN KINGS

Most ancient Kings claimed to be not only God's representative but actual, physical sons of God – dating at least as far back as the Sumerian Kings who traced their physical lineage to "the gods". And if you think it is accidental that the words 'sun' and 'son' are almost identical – I invite you to reconsider, and will point out that English was the latest European language created and that it almost certainly was done so with intention.

The physical Sun – the star that is placed at the center of our planetary system – is the most constant, enduring and dependable thing in the physical world. It sustains life, makes life possible. What better physical object than the Sun to exemplify the physical presence of spirit – the part of us that endures/exists beyond physical death? Like the physical Sun warming the earth, you are expressing your feelings out into the environment around you – which are then felt in the hearts of the people around you. Giving is what you do.

OPEN UP YOUR HEART

The best way to keep your Heart Chakra operating as intended is by giving. The opening of your Heart allows for a 2-way flow to take place. As your Heart is opened, your gifts are now able to be given away. And of course the same opening allows you to receive love as well. Fear is perhaps the greatest challenge to opening one's Heart and so proactively looking at and addressing your fears – a supreme act of *cour*age – will begin the process of getting your Heart into a state where it can open fully.

Chapter 7

CROWN CHAKRA – JUPITER

"I am Connected to Source..."

We now move up to the Crown Chakra. And I'm sure the first question on your mind is, "how did we jump from 4 to 7?" The idea here is that, being the product of two components – spirit and matter – and as physical energy symbolically emanates from the earth, and moving upwards enters through our Root Chakra, our Spiritual energy emanates from 'heaven' and travels downward entering through our Crown. Thus we are at the receiving end of two streams of energy which converge in the Heart. If you have ever looked at different images of crowns, you may have noticed that many – similar to the scales of a female pine cone or the petals of flowers – have pointy parts angled upward and outward from the circle of the head. This is to symbolize openness and receptivity to Spiritual energy.

JUPITER – KING OF THE GODS

The crown of the earthly King symbolizes the unique connection that he has to the divine. Of course, you having your own Crown Chakra is analogous to you having your own direct contact with Source. Therefore we see in modern times the disappearance of Kings and the concept of only one special person having contact with the divine whom we must exalt, honor, and revere as unique and special, giving way to the idea of each of us seeking (and finding!) the God within.

Keeping your Crown open is the way to maintain your Spiritual connection. And we do this by keeping our *awareness* on that connection and the unseen world it connects us to. So often in our day-to-day lives physical activities and the information discerned by the physical senses tend to dominate our minds. The practice of meditating twice a day, or facing towards Mecca and praying five times a day, or saying Grace before every meal are all examples of conscious, purposeful, physical activities that call our attention back to the Spiritual side of life.

PAIRS

As we begin our exploration of the upper three Chakras we now may notice a pairing – 1 and 7, 2 and 6, 3 and 5. In this instance we notice that the 1st and 7th Chakras are both *connectors* - the Root Chakra representing our connection to the earth – our physical connection – the Crown Chakra represent our connection to spirit, the Universe, God or our own Higher-Self – that part of us that existed before our physical life began and which will continue after it is ended. Many words are used by different people to denote the Spiritual realm – the cosmos, the universe, Heaven, the quantum field, the space that exists between the parts of atoms, the divine. Call it what you will, the essence of this realm is that it exists outside of the perception of our five physical senses. It is the unseen world. There is perhaps no definitive scientific proof for its existence. But the mere awareness of ourselves as individuals with thoughts and feelings is evidence of its existence.

Thought and awareness are nonphysical phenomena. The changing feelings in a relationship between lovers is a non-physical phenomenon and yet with very real and physically obvious results. And this underscores the most important realization about the relationship between spirit and matter, a point which is at the heart of most if not all religious and Spiritual practices and even new ideas in science – that all matter is informed, motivated, supported and even created in the unseen or Spiritual realm. I have used the word *awareness* several times here to make the point that the Spiritual/energetic realm is there whether you are aware of its existence or not and so *becoming* aware of it by focusing your attention upon it in any given moment of time is key to consciously including it in your life. The Crown Chakra symbolizes your connection to this realm.

EGO

As Eckhart Tolle points out[8] – standing just inside the gate of your consciousness to make sure that no Spiritual energy or *awareness* gets in, lies the ego – the egoic, thinking mind which serves us by drawing a distinction between ourselves and everything else. This is one reason the Spiritual dimension is often forgotten – because as individual, *physical* aspects of the one Great Spirit – we must be able to identify where we are and where we are not. Who we are and who we are not. This is the nature of individuation – one must identify as an individual. The problem with so many of us is that we forget to also identify with our Spiritual half. Some will say that Spiritual amnesia is necessary – for if spirit is everywhere and brings awareness of everything it would be over-whelming for us to have all that information and all the answers. It would also make life incurably boring, for if we knew exactly why we were here and how long we had to be here we would lose the opportunity for the wisdom that comes from figuring things out for ourselves, as well as the opportunity to cherish or blatantly squander our time – it is a free-will universe after all.

So, we seemingly must forget our Spiritual connection in order to focus upon establishing a distinct identity. And then ironically many of us will spend the rest of our lives missing that connection and attempting to re-establish that connection.

Our Spiritual nature then, for better or worse is pared-down after we enter into the physical dimension. We must first learn the rules of the physical world. And as so often happens in the West, children's Spiritual connec-tion begins to atrophy as they age. Indeed scientist tell us that at age seven (which incidentally is related to the movement of Saturn – god of form and definition, and the most reality-based of the gods) children will experi-ence a developmental shift so that their minds are less focused on the imaginary world and more able to grasp material realities. What seems to be lacking in our culture is a simultaneous cultivation of our Spiritual nature while we are learning reading, writing and arithmetic on a full-time basis by age 7 (or younger!) The time spent cultivating our Spiritual nature for the average American is somewhere between none and almost none.

PHILOSOPHY

Regardless of our level of awareness of this realm, it continues to exist. It is as constant and as certain as your heartbeat – always there. Attitudes, religious beliefs and worldviews are three examples of things that are unseen, very often unnoticed and usually unexamined but which play a decisive role in determining your physical reality and how you perceive it – motivating our actions, choices and coloring our responses to the challenges of this life. In astrology the planet Jupiter represents the big picture – including ideas of religion, law, philosophy and guiding principles. Jupiter is the "King of the Gods" occupying his throne on the top of Mount Olympus – which offers him this higher perspective. So too, our Crown Chakra represents belief systems, wide perspectives and points of view which shape the rest of our experience. On the energetic level, the ratio of Spiritual information allowed in to Egoic control over our awareness tells us how far along the Spiritual development curve we are. Just as the ratio of new information from outside our daily experience vs. the amount of same-old information we receive every day is a good indication of how open-minded a person we may be.

ANOTHER BRICK IN THE WALL

Organized religion has done its part to reinforce the egoic barrier between you and your Source. The Catholic Church with their priests to whom you must go to for confession is an example of how most westerners were fooled into believing they needed a *third*-party (3rd Chakra/Saturn/the Establishment) to make that connection on their behalf. It's as if some sort of Spiritual lobotomy was performed en mass as Europeans and later Americans were convinced they were unable to make direct contact with God. Prayers seemed to have been the only allowable exception. Understanding the nature of prayer helps us see how and why it was encouraged and allowed. Prayer is a masculine act – an act of reaching out towards God. Its opposite, or companion, may be called meditation – a feminine allowance to be penetrated by God. In other words you don't have to do anything to connect with spirit you simply *stop doing* and allow the *awareness* of spirit (which is existing in all places at all times) to possess you. Imagine God/Creator/Source surrounding you and wanting to take part in your life and actively reaching out towards you (rather than passively sitting in heaven waiting to be petitioned for favors). Jesus phrased this masculine Spiritual process as "Behold, I stand at the door and knock". The door is the feminine/receptive entrance to your awareness – your Crown Chakra – Jesus representing the Spiritual energy wanting to connect with you consciously. Recall from the Radiance Sutra quoted at the beginning of this book – incarnation and immortality are *passionate* for each other. God is not passively waiting and hoping to be asked in. Spirit and the awareness of the Spiritual dimension is surrounding and penetrating us even when we are not paying attention.

The stories of Zeus (the Greek version of Jupiter) paint an entirely different picture of god/source/spirit – an active, masculine and passionate god constantly coming down to earth to impregnate one maiden or another. This is symbolic of not just the desire but the *need* of spirit to penetrate matter, just as matter needs to be penetrated by spirit. Christianity actually reversed the mythology and eliminated the proactive nature of spirit and the receptive nature of humanity by taking away God's unsolicited active nature (except when punishing or judging) and casting us humans in the role of supplicants having to petition or beg God to become active in our lives – rather than simply allowing it to be so.

Not to downplay the importance and necessity of the masculine quality in us to pray and/or reach out for what we want. Rather to point out that most of what we think about God/spirit is based on an incomplete story. It is said that half-lies are worse than lies, because they have enough truth in them to keep you thinking they are genuine. The Crown Chakra asks us to add meditation back into the equation in order to be balanced and to honor the masculine nature of spirit and its desire to penetrate us.

CHANNEL 7

Flashes of brilliance and inspiration are examples of being penetrated by this unseen Force. Another is channeling – a practice where one is able to put their own consciousness or ego aside and allow another's to penetrate their being and speak through them. Many are familiar with the works of Esther Hicks who channels Abraham, Darryl Anka who channels Bashar, Jane Roberts who channeled Seth and of course the grandfather of American New Age thought, Pisces Edgar Cayce – the Sleeping Prophet who would lay down, go to sleep and then begin speaking – offering guidance and solutions to his clients of which he was completely unaware. While these examples are well-known, the fact is each of us is a channel for spirit to come through. The average person may not do it regularly, consciously or professionally – but most if not all of us have experienced a moment when we knew something we did not know the moment before. Very often it can be in times of crisis when a solution (often life-saving) is immediately needed and in a flash you know exactly what to do. For me personally it manifested many times when I was in deep conversation with my young child dealing with emotional and developmental crises. Suddenly in the midst of conversing I would somehow magically have the perfect words come out of my mouth. Words, ideas or concepts that I had never thought of before. Wisdom I had had no access to before the moment I needed it. We have all experienced moments like this when our ego will jump out of the way and let spirit come through.

LUCK, SAGITTARIUS AND PISCES

In astrology Jupiter represents expansion, abundance, growth and good fortune. One of our favorite moments in life is when we experience synchronicity – the seemingly magical intersection of events or people who you were just thinking of moments before and then they suddenly show up. Serendipity is another word used often to describe this art of being in the right place at the right time.

Your clear connection to spirit facilitates this experience. And the more connected you are – the more often you open the door and consciously allow spirit into your life – the more often this occurs. Pisces and Sagittarius – the two signs ruled by Jupiter seem to have more than their share of luck. But we all are able to manifest miracles – large or small – the more so as we cultivate our connection to Source. Another fascinating behavior found in many Sagittarius and Pisces people is that they will duplicate this Spiritual reality of connectedness on the physical level by meeting as many other people as possible. Social butterflies, networkers and even broadcasters will typically all share a strong Jupiter in their astrological charts.

INTERCONNECTED

Another wonderful result that comes from having Spiritual awareness is that when you realize you are connected to spirit, you then realize that everyone else is connected to spirit. You then understand yourself to be interconnected to everyone and you share the same Spiritual heritage with everyone else and you are therefore related to everyone else. I believe the current breakdown of civility at all levels in our culture is tied directly to the absence of this *awareness* of inter-connection. I say awareness because, again it is a free-will universe and we are all free to embrace or ignore this reality. Our cultural, educational and religious institutions all contribute to our ignorance. However we do find ourselves shocked back into this awareness of our interconnectedness during times of crisis – hurricanes, floods, earthquakes and other disasters will bring out the latent connectedness in us – as strangers will help each other out when the facade of material security is stripped away and our eyes are opened to our common humanity. Jupiter sees clearly the whole picture – not just your personal piece of it – as he sits on top of Mount Olympus or at the top of your body in the Crown Chakra. Becoming aware of this connection and realizing your interconnectedness is the first step as spirit symbolically descends into your body.

PUT ON YOUR CROWN

An inactive Crown Chakra is a common feature in our busy culture. Taking a moment to breathe consciously is the most natural way to disconnect from the busyness of the material world. If you can stop *thinking* for a moment and instead *focus* your mind upon your breath, you are on your way to waking up to the unseen side of life. Going a step further and taking a few or several minutes to stop thinking is even more powerful. Continuing on this track you can also stop thinking at certain points during the day. Driving and walking for example are two common activities that do not require us to think about our job, or relationships or politics or plans for the future while we are doing them. The more often we *catch* ourselves thinking – the more often we can disengage that side of our mind and allow the unseen side of life to show itself to us.

Chapter 6

BROW CHAKRA – THE MOON

"...which Inspires me..."

The Brow Chakra or *third eye*, as it has become known, is the seat of our sixth sense – the ability to receive/perceive non-physical information from the world around us. Just as a physical eye receives physical information – light – and relays that information to our brain and gives us something to think about, the third eye receives and sends information of a different sort to our mind – vibes, feelings, reading between the lines and sensing another's feelings and intentions even when their words say something different. Picking up on these non-physical cues, the 3rd Eye *sees* the energy that underlies the physical world.

The astrological Moon corresponds to the 6th Chakra. Long regarded as a feminine and motherly symbol, the Moon as well as the number 6 and intuition are linked via expressions such as "women's intuition" and "the 6th Sense". Women are naturally more attuned to the feminine side of being, just as men are naturally attuned to the masculine. Saying that women are more intuitive than men, though a fairly disempowering attitude for a man to take, does bear some truth.

Biologically, women are constructed to be receptive. And so the perception/receptivity that is associated with the 3rd Eye may come more easily to the average woman. It is possible of course for men to be receptive/perceptive just as women have masculine qualities, but after a few years of cultural conditioning – as well as being naturally focused on expressing energy rather than receiving it – a man will typically have to work consciously and intentionally to develop this faculty.

SENSITIVITY

The Moon in astrological symbolism represents our emotional nature. How we relate to others and what our own emotional needs are are represented by the Moon. Emotional sensitivity and intuitive perception run on a scale within the human race with some of us being more sensitive than others. Emotion and intuition are linked, as one is either open or not. And if you are open to the non-physical world of energy and forces then emotions are a part of that package. You cannot separate the two.

The Moon also symbolizes the night – the time when we lay our conscious mind to rest and our unconscious takes over in the form of dreams. Men and women are generally more focused on the physical world while awake. Mouths to feed, jobs to do, etc. – all call our focus and attention away from the unseen world. But just as the Moon spends almost as much time visible during the day as it does during the night – we don't tend to notice the Moon during the day unless we are looking in the right direction – usually by happenstance, so too, during the day the unseen world will often lie just beneath our awareness until, in a flash, we get an intuitive burst – sometimes a "gut feeling" that tells us to pay attention to something we may be overlooking.* Very often it can be a flash of insight like the proverbial "light bulb" going on in our head or a moment of inspiration. These sudden, unexpected messages are not random or senseless – rather they are profound *insights* – "seeing in-ward" – by which you are accessing information that your five senses cannot.

IMAGINATION

Sometimes during our waking hours we will slip into a 6th Chakra state of mind. The words *imagination* and *daydream* are used to denote this slipping into the other world during waking hours. The word 'imagination' is not nearly as insignificant or fanciful as we may have been led to believe. The word literally means to have an 'image' put 'in' to your mind. Put there by whom? It is contact with our own higher self/higher mind via the Crown Chakra that takes shape in the thoughts of our imagination.

Daydreaming describes the often unplanned phenomena of disconnecting from your awareness of the world around you, turning off those five senses and drifting into

---

*the Moon corresponds to the stomach in astrology

the realm of the 6th Chakra. It is as if the unconscious mind has an important message that can't wait for night-time. Again, this is highly valuable information coming to you via the Sixth Sense – so valuable that it interrupts your conscious state of mind, drawing your attention to what is more important to spirit than what you may be focused on at the moment. Also there is the simple need to give your conscious mind a break from time to time. Many of us are in highly production-oriented jobs – working eight or more hours a day, five, six or seven days a week, and constantly engaging the rational, logical side of the brain. Daydreaming is your mind's need to disconnect the rational side of the mind before it blows a fuse! Coffee breaks, union breaks and recess at school are all designed to give our conscious minds a break. By meditating or simply staring into space during a coffee break one may actually regain balance between left/right brain – masculine/feminine, conscious/unconscious.

ESCAPE

One by-product of a left-brain dominant culture, which does not honor or allow daydreaming, imagination or any other kind of constructive exercise of psychic abil-ities, is the exaggerated need for escape. Drugs and alcohol serve to slow the rational thinking function and allow the other parts of our psyche to come to the fore-front. Another word for alcohol is 'spirits'. The downside of alcohol-induced escapism is of course that the 'spirit' coming through – those unconscious components of our psyche – is now out of control and liable to do damage to persons, relationships and property as well as to the very brain-cells that are responsible for processing the logical, rational information. Self-sabotage at its finest as the unconscious side fights back against its being relegated to second-class status!

BEHIND THE SCENES

Any student of music knows that there comes a point when in the midst of practicing a certain piece – usually after a seemingly endless period of frustrating repetition – that one must walk away from the piece. And when returning to practice the next day they find that they have somehow improved during that space of time even though they have not been 'doing' anything! This applies to learning of all kinds, problem solving, and arguments between lovers. When we disengage the left-side of the brain, the right-side is allowed to do its work – unseen, unnoticed, and yet incredibly powerful, useful and necessary. The Spiritual/unseen component of our lives enriches us in ways beyond our wildest 'dreams'.

TRAINING THE MIND

Carl Jung, the eminent Swiss psychologist who's Moon was in Taurus – the astrological sign in which the Moon is said to be 'exalted' or strengthened – created a form of therapy/self-help known as Active Imagination. This is where one purposely and consciously enters into an internal dialogue between the conscious egoic mind and the other, less conscious aspects of one's personality. By consciously and purposely engaging this realm of one's being rather than allowing it to remain unconscious, un-accessed and liable to show up at the most inconvenient times, we become more balanced and aware of our inner world. The well-known "Freudian Slip" is an example of how our unconscious can come bursting through into our experience in an unexpected, unpredictable and often embarrassing manner.

Active Imagination and other tools such as Dream Journaling train us and help to bring more and more of these unconscious aspects of our being into consciousness where we may put them to use. One need not be a professional psychic to have an active relationship with the unseen side of life.

THE VOICE OF GOD

Being non-physical, spirit or God does not speak English, French, Japanese or any other language. God/spirit is a non-physical phenomenon and therefore communicates in a non-physical manner. This is what inspiration is. The word 'inspire' means to experience the 'spirit-in' you. This can also be likened to the saying of Jesus – "the kingdom of heaven lies within". Christianity takes this concept and turns it into an external entity – "the Holy Spirit" – something you may or may not get (by being filled with the holy spirit). Rather it is seen by esotericists as an *inner* resource – naturally possessed by us all – that may be either embraced or lie untapped. Again, we see Christianity attempting to change the script – this time by portraying the intuitive ability as something outside of you that may be *given* to you versus a faculty that you already possess, ready to be cultivated. The phrase "god-given ability" is a patriarchal misportrayal of this concept as it actually refers to something we are all *born with* (mother/moon) and does not require an external figure to *give* it to us.

THE ASTROLOGICAL SIGN CANCER

Not everyone will rely upon or cultivate their intuition as much as a professional psychic, but the ability is there for all of us. Those who are born under the sign of Cancer and especially those born with the Moon in Cancer may find that they have a very hard time turning their inner voice off. Many "6th sensitive" people today suffer from an acute intuitive faculty coupled with living too close to too many people experiencing emotional upheavals too often.

As an astrologer I have counseled many clients – both men and women – who find they have no explanation for what is happening to them when they experience other's feelings as acutely as their own. And in a culture and environment where the intuition is not honored and in some places not permitted, it is little wonder that so many of us are cracking up. Our minds are not getting what they need. It is worth noting here that if a person is artificially kept from dreaming they will literally go crazy after a matter of days. This non-physical information and the need of the mind to engage in dreams, and process other non-physically sourced information is crucial to our mental health. There are in fact two sides of the brain, or two mental processes – the left and right sides corresponding to rational, logical thought and intuition/creativity. I mentioned in the last chapter that there is a natural pairing between upper and lower chakras. Here we see the relationship between 2nd and 6th, where the creative center (2nd Chakra) is fed by thoughts from the creative side of the brain and the unconscious part of the mind (6th Chakra).

Our two corresponding planets – Venus and the Moon – are our only two strictly feminine planets symbolizing (amongst other things) the mother's (Moon/6th Chakra) womb (Venus/2nd chakra).

When we consider these 2 Chakras as symbolic of Creativity and Intuition and their relationship to mothering – it is important to know that from the perspective of the 3rd Eye there are no *accidents*. In our example in Chapter 2 of the peanut butter cups – the old TV commercial shows two men accidentally bumping into each other and combining their two different snacks. But what appears to be an accident to the rational mind can be a carefully orchestrated event from the level of the Brow Chakra. Some part of you 'knows' to take this next turn although you don't know why or what it may lead to. Some part of you also knows who is your mate. Many of us have 'unknowingly' selected mates with whom we procreate but do not stay with for very long. Spirit or the Higher Mind may have altogether different ideas about who should father or bear your child than your conscious, rational mind does. And of course many 'accidents' of a procreative nature turn out to be the greatest blessings in our lives.

Other so called 'accidents' always contain a message – it's another way of the 3rd Eye calling your attention to something you've been overlooking. Injuries, car accidents and illnesses are often means by which your higher self will force 'you' – your egoic mind, that is – to pay attention to behaviors, beliefs and habits that may no longer serve you. The wise among us will always look for the message hidden in a traumatic event.

Feminine phenomena – creativity and emotions – tend to run in cycles of high to low and back to high just as the Moon constantly *cycles* between New and Full and back to New – rather than *maintaining* at a constant level. That is the masculine Sun's job. It hardly needs mentioning that a woman's menstrual cycle is a direct manifestation of the cyclical nature that belongs to the feminine. And so we see the Sun and the Moon representing the two main energies – just as Kundalini is represented by two snakes (masculine and feminine) – head and heart are the two most powerful internal forces we seek to reconcile in our own experience as men and women. The integration of head and heart – of cyclical lunar rhythms with constant solar rhythms – remains one of the greatest challenges of our modern Human family. The key of course lies in honoring each as valid, important and central to our existence.

BROW

For our Cancerians and other lunar types, having an abundance of emotional/Spiritual awareness is often a disabling condition. For those on the other extreme – where the Brow Chakra is inactive – we often find a lack of sensitivity to other's feelings as well as an atrophying of their own imagination. In the first instance, for someone experiencing Spiritual or emotional overload – regularly taking time "away from the maddening crowd" is an absolute requirement. On the other hand, those whose sensitivity and imagination are below average can use dream-journaling or active imagination exercises to begin to 'see' the unseen side of life. And of course learning how to listen to other people is the first step in cultivating more emotional sensitivity.

MOTHER – THE ARCHETYPE

So far I have used specific, individual people (factual and fictional) as examples for each Chakra. The 6th Chakra however represents awareness of that which is not seen but rather *felt*. So I cannot *show* you an example. What I can do is draw your inner eye towards that which is already within you. And so I offer not one, but an infinite number of beings who have and continue to embody this energy.

For many, the best examples are our own mother or grandmothers. For others it may be a woman – or possibly a man – who embodied the nurturing and caretaking nature of a mother when you were young, sick, injured, distraught, out of luck or otherwise in need of someone to hold you in an accepting, nurturing and non-judgmental manner.

Many Native American cultures regard the Moon as "Grandmother". In this case the Moon can be likened to the grandmother who sees you from a bit of a distance, where mother may be too close to have an objective perspective – someone who *knows* you better than anyone else because they are intuitively hearing/seeing the parts of you that others do not. Combining insight with emotional sensitivity and loving acceptance shows us the Brow Chakra operateing at its best in the people around us.

Chapter 5

THROAT CHAKRA – MERCURY

"...to Share My Truth..."

Mercury is the busiest of the Gods, wearing more hats than all the others combined. Mercury and the Throat Chakra symbolize the rational, logical mind, thought, speech, learning, teaching, science, medicine, mirth, magic, mischief, craftsmanship, skill and all forms of commerce, exchange and communication. Just as mercury the element is also known as *quicksilver*, Mercury the god speeds through the world delivering messages from Jupiter at the top of Mount Olympus to us Mortals here on Earth in a flash – so too, your thoughts and mind work at lightning speed. Amateur astrologers often associate Mercury and the throat solely with communication – not realizing that speech and communication are merely the end products of thought. It is in that millisecond between thought and speech that we see the mythological journey of Mercury from Mount Olympus to Earth enacted in ourselves – symbolizing the movement from non-physical thought or spirit into matter/speech. The Throat represents the easiest way for most of us to perform this incredible feat of Magic – the turning of Energy into Matter. Remember, thought is of the same nature as spirit. That is to say it is non-physical. It is energy and when you put a thought into words you are literally *materializing* it. Sound is the movement of physical molecules of air and the resulting vibration of your physical eardrums. Energy into matter – just like that. (And you thought you were just whistlin' Dixie!)

THE MIDDLE-MAN

Mercury moves not only between Heaven and Earth, he also serves as the ferryman taking dead souls across the River Styx from the land of the living to the Underworld. His middle-man status is further reflected in words we use today such as *mer*chant, *mer*chandise and com*mer*ce –merchants being the middle men and women between producers and consumers. Mercury's day – Wednesday (Miercoles in Spanish) is the *middle* of the week as is the letter M in the middle of the alphabet. The astrological symbol for Mercury is comprised of three parts – the symbols for Moon, Sun and Earth – and the Throat Chakra is, of course, located between our two strongest forces – head and heart, Moon and Sun.

SAY IT LOUD

The all-important and powerful aspect of speech and use of the Throat is one of the most underestimated and neglected aspects of our world. Children are constantly being shushed by parents and teachers. Men (generally) have been ignoring women's voices as a matter of cultural norm for centuries. As it turns out, we are all actually designed to speak to one another – to hear and be heard. You do not need a throat to speak to yourself. Nor do you need one to talk to God. The function and therefore the prime purpose of the Throat Chakra is so that we may speak to each other. To share our wisdom, our knowledge, our feelings and our truth. This concept of verbal sharing can also be extrapolated into sharing as a primary state of being. We share the Earth with each other, for example. We share resources and experiences as well as thoughts. And so speaking your *Truth* becomes an essential task – for two reasons. The first is to say what we know because there is something inside that must be expressed. The other side of the coin is that there is somebody that *needs* to hear what you have to say. No one has all the answers. No one is an island. We are designed to give and receive (share) information. And because we are all in separate bodies with different skills and challenges, different genetics, different personalities and thoughts – we each have a unique understanding of Life (the expression of spirit in matter). And sometimes the sharing of your Truth is just what someone else needs to hear. I remember when my chart was first read by an astrologer, he told me, "Johnny, the practice that best serves those of your astrological sign is detachment". I then asked what detachment was and the astrologer attempted to define it for me. I was, however, still uncertain after the explanation, so he said, "Read some Buddhism – that will help you understand." So I read some Buddhist teachings on detachment but still, I was not certain. It wasn't until several years later that I came across the books of Eckhart

Tolle. And when I read one certain page in his book where he talks about detachment, I got it! Eckhart Tolle had used just the right words that I could relate to and understand, and I read them at just the right moment – perhaps when I was ready to hear them. So too, do you have some "Pearl of Wisdom" – some Truth – that you have discovered for yourself to be meaningful and true that you are destined to share with someone who really needs to hear it. Because sharing is what we do. And the more truth we share the more enriched our world becomes. The exchange of ideas and information supports our mental and Spiritual development in much the same way the exchange of money, goods and services supports our physical being. The more truth we share the more enriched our world becomes.

PUZZLED

It is as if we are all building a giant jigsaw puzzle and each of us is given a piece to fit in. Anyone who has built a jigsaw puzzle knows how really slow-going it is at first, but the more pieces that are played, the clearer the picture becomes and the easier it is to play the remaining pieces. This is how human consciousness works as well – the more of us there are sharing our Truth the clearer the "big picture" becomes and the easier it is for each of us – as well as future generations – to move further ahead. Just think of how much more you know today than you did a decade ago. Or consider your parents and how much further along you are technologically, possibly also intellectually and certainly also in the options you have available to you in the 21st century that simply were not in existence in the 20th century. And in terms of our Spiritual development we all like to think we are evolving as a species into a more advanced form. If the technological and Spiritual giants who came before us – such as Edison and Tesla, Jesus and the Buddha – had not shared – then we would all be much further behind than where we are now.

The picture is not complete unless everyone fits their piece. Sharing our Truth is the primary means of expanding Consciousness. Each of us having our own subjective experience of being "Spirit in Matter" and the more of these experiences being shared, the more we understand about the nature of being Human. By sharing and learning from others' sharing, we grow our own awareness and the awareness of others. It is a cascading effect that ripples out from one person to thousands, millions, even billions of others.

SPEAKING TRUTH

Your Truth – your voice, is potent and powerful stuff. Just as the messenger god, Mercury is bringing a message down to Earth from Jupiter, we may also bring a message down from our Crown Chakra at times – our connection to our own higher mind, Universal Consciousness or God. And so we may take the suggestion of author Don Miguel Ruiz to heart "Be Impeccable With your Word" – because it is powerful magic.[9] The power of sound is the power of creation itself. Song and speech are at the heart of almost every creation myth on the planet. In the Biblical creation myth God *speaks* the entire world into being. For mere mortals such as you and I, it works the exact same way. Remember I mentioned how the upper and lower chakras are paired? The 5th Chakra is paired with the 3rd – the *manifesting* Chakra. As we speak (or write) our intentions they take physical shape. That physical shape or sound wave has an impact on the world around us. Once spoken or written, thoughts and desires can then begin to attract other physical components – people, money, resources – and take shape as actual things.

THE JOKER

Mercury is also known as the Trickster God. A handful of comedians who do more than just tell jokes grace us by speaking Truth and using humor to make it more palatable. After all, it is much easier to hear about our own shortcomings if we are shown not only how ridiculous they are but that we share these shortcomings with the vast majority of other people. The Trickster God's main purpose is to make a fool of those who are taking themselves too seriously or are too blind to see their own faults. Tricksters have a way of taking us down a notch when we get a swollen, egotistical head.

BACK AND FORTH

Another example of Mercury's go-between role is in dream journaling. Writing down information from the non-physical realm into a physical form is an example of Mercury going to the other side and coming back. Science has described for us the *corpus callosum* – the barrier between the left and right hemispheres of the brain – and the value of having multiple connections between the two. Mercury's journey is the mythological counterpart to the scientifically understood process of creating links across your *corpus callosum* – bringing right and left halves of the brain into greater coherence by learning to combine your logical mind with your creative mind.

Dream-journaling is a purposeful act driven by the will and desire to make conscious and physical that which is unconscious or energy. Making dreams into reality begins with writing down those dreams after which they may take on a life of their own and begin to aggregate more energy or form. And, as most of us know, if we do not remember our dreams or write down our brilliant flashes of inspiration and other insights from the 6th Chakra, they may simply evaporate – disappearing back into the unconscious.

The brilliant and possibly the most famous mercurial character in our modern world, Gemini Paul McCartney, describes his inspiration for the song *Yesterday* – one of, if not the most widely recorded and performed songs ever. He had dreamt the song while sleeping one night and woke up with the tune in his head – at which point he immediately went to the piano to translate it into physical reality. Again, what is needed is a conscious and purposeful act – getting up and writing it down in this case – on the part of you or I to pull our dreams and inspirations into physical being in order to make them 'real'.

IN SERVICE

Mercury is there to serve the higher-mind and the will (the Sun). He must be purposefully guided towards your goals or he will create all kinds of mischief if left to his own devices. The power of positive thinking and conscious languaging are two examples of ways we may embrace Mercury as the servant of the will rather than as the truant, prankster or juvenile delinquent. The two signs ruled by Mercury, Gemini and Virgo – represent the wild and free adolescent (Gemini) and the servant (Virgo) symbolizing these two aspects of the Mercury principle. Mercury represents the thief and con-man when his clever mind is not guided into creative and useful activity. If you are a Harry Potter fan you will recall the Weasley *twins* as the pranksters of the class who not only become "high-school dropouts" but then channel the power of their clever minds into a successful 'joke' shop – illustrating the principle of harnessing your youthful enthusiasm and mind into service to your Self.[10]

MAGIC

The wizards and witches of literature and fairy tale – from King Arthur's Merlin, to Gandalf of Lord of the Rings, to the witches of Shakespeare's Macbeth, to the characters in Harry Potter are symbolizing the power of the spoken word that we all possess. In Fairy Tales, wizards and witches will cast a spell – combining 3rd and 5th Chakras by speaking a powerful set of words (an incantation) and channeling that power through a magic wand – a physical instrument made of the stuff of the earth – crystals and wood. Interesting when you realize that one of the first things we learn how to do at school is to *spell*. Your words are magic indeed – you weren't just told this growing up but you can see for yourself how you can impact the thoughts and actions of others with your words if you have not noticed already. Two of the best examples from recent history are Adolph Hitler and Martin Luther King, Jr. Hitler created an entire world at war with the power of his voice. He never pulled a trigger, ironically, until the end of the war when he took his own life. Instead he inspired and motivated through his speeches a great many people to pull triggers. Martin Luther King, Jr. likewise inspired a great many people while he lived and continues to do so decades after his passing by combining an absolute mastery of the English language with moral force, an incredible strength of will and Love.

Just as Hitler and Martin Luther King, Jr. were able to evoke the worst and best in human nature, so too are you influencing those with whom you speak – evoking their light side or their dark side. Our choice of words takes on even more significance when we see their far-reaching effects. As a side note it should be pointed out that who you choose to listen to is a vastly important choice to make as well, for your ears are also part of the Throat Chakra – in fact all 5 senses are used to feed the 5th Chakra and the conscious, logical thinking mind – and so the receiving of information is just as important as the delivering it.

HIGH MAGIC

The Judeo/Christian Mythos shows us (for those who have eyes to see) that Moses and Jesus were actually *magicians* or as they were know in those days "Magi". This is not to denigrate these two figures to the level of modern-day magicians who pull rabbits out of hats and do card tricks – rather, to elevate your (dear reader's) awareness of what Magic is really all about. Manipulating the material world by first affecting a shift on the non-physical plane is true magic – from turning a staff into a serpent, to restoring sight to the blind, to setting an intention on a vision board. Jesus' actual name was something like Jeshua. It's shortening to a 5-letter word in the Bible is one more example of how esoteric information was encoded into the Bible for those "who have eyes to see", as so many of our 5-letter words embody the 5th Chakra's essence: magic, skill, craft, Jesus, Moses, learn, teach, speak, mirth, laugh, trick, think, write...

GOT A MATCH?

Magic can also be understood to be having a knowledge of physical forces so deep that you may do things that appear to be magical. A full grasp of Universal and Physical principles via our mind – symbolizing science at its best – allows one to do things the unschooled cannot. Matches are an example of things that were first thought to be magic – the ability to create fire on a stick is an amazing trick – until one learns that it is simply a matter of combining the right ingredients in the right way and putting them on a dry stick. Science is seemingly 'discovering' Spiritual truths to be physical realities every week these days as new technology allows us to see what the Magi have known for ages.

GEMINI AND VIRGO

Mercury rules the two astrological signs Gemini and Virgo. Remember – you don't actually have to be a Gemini or Virgo to have an active Throat Chakra. The planet Mercury could be making contact with any number of significant points in your astrological chart and you would qualify as 'Mercurial'. Mercury people tend to be the thinkers of the world – always running things over in their head. This doesn't mean that they are necessarily smart, wise or educated (though many are). It means that they strive to make logical sense of the world around them and so they are *thinking* about things that are happening – perhaps a bit more than the average person. Prolific speakers will also have a strong Mercury in their charts, from inspirational verbal masters such as MLK Jr., to the guy at the party who sends everyone within earshot into a stunned silence while he treats them to a sample of "diarrhea of the mouth".

BILL HICKS

To close this chapter I offer my favorite joke from the late, great comedian, Bill Hicks. Bill said, "How come we never hear a positive drug story on the news? The news is supposed to be objective but all we ever hear is, "'Today a young man on acid thought he could fly and jumped out of a second story window and died. What a tragedy.' What a jerk!", Bill says. "How about this for a positive drug story? 'Today, a young man on acid realized that all matter is merely energy slowed down to a dense vibration. That we are all one consciousness experiencing itself subjectively. There is no Death. Life is a Dream and we are the Imagination of our Selves...Here's Tom, with the weather.'"

Funny. True. "We are all one consciousness experiencing itself subjectively" is reference to both the common source which we all came from – God/Spirit/Creator/Universe – and to our own individual existence and identity here on the earth. We are each one unique, subjective expression and experience of what it is to be spirit in a human body. One reason why there are so many of us – so many different bodies – is that the expansion of consciousness requires more than one point of view. Otherwise there would be severely limited expansion and understanding. So each one of us not only has our own unique body with our own unique history and personality and points of view and challenges and gifts but also each possesses a unique connection to the Source – with a unique Spiritual mission or purpose for being here.

Getting back to the assertion I made back in Chapter 1 – where I mentioned that there is a powerful Spiritual purpose behind having your physical body – this is where we see that need and purpose for the physical body. Spirit needs you in your body with your unique personality, gifts, challenges, etc. to have your unique, subjective experience. *Your* contribution to the overall big picture can only be accomplished by you. Your life is indeed precious – a one and only, that will ever be. You are the only one who can bring your gift to the world.

CHAPTER 8 – BRING IT

*"I am Here to Create and Establish Things
That Encourage Love; I am Connected to Source, Which
Inspires Me to Share My Truth With The World."*

The last stage of our symbolic journey through the Chakras is down from the Throat into the Heart. Without this final step, our Spiritual ideals, dreams, inspiration and vision lack a connection to the real world. Professors and other intellectuals are often accused of living in 'Ivory Towers' – a reference to being 'above it all', above the material plane – preferring to live a life insulated from the messiness that comes from actual application of mental theory into physical practice. The expression "living in your head" is another way we often phrase the disconnect that results from not allowing yourself to fully engage on the dense, material Earth plane. Spirit, however, craves contact with the physical world, just as the physical world yearns for spirit. The energetic journey is completed by the descent of Spiritual energy into the Heart where it makes contact with the material energy having risen from the earth. The journey may be complete, however the story is just beginning!

The combination of spirit and matter in the heart initiates the alchemical process where by combining these two elements you become the child (the creation) of your own consciousness. Self-actualizing and fulfilling your potential requires that you activate each component of your energy system and then operate from a place of integration – the Heart.

THE WORLD

The last of our 26 word sentence are the words "with the world". When one looks below at this visual depiction of what we have been reading, we see the physical energy rising up from the earth and entering the Root Chakra, and Spiritual energy traveling down from heaven and entering through the Crown Chakra. As the two energies meet and combine in the Heart Chakra, they symbolically mix as if being stirred in a cauldron, where they then may be sent out into the world.

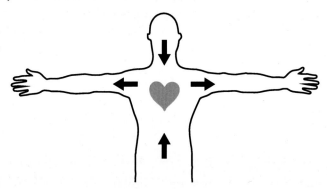

If this image looks familiar it is because it is one of the most prevalent symbols in our culture – the cross. The cross has been found in cultures much older than ours and from all around the planet. Christianity is only the latest religion to adopt this powerful symbol. Setting religion aside, we see the cross for what it symbolizes – the flow of energy into a human body, the combination of this energy in the heart and then the releasing or giving away or gifting of the combined energy – your own unique blend of forces. You truly are a one-of-a-kind gift to the world.

"The World" is whomever we come into contact with – the receiver of our gift. Friends and family are obvious examples. "The World" also includes strangers you come into contact with, people you see regularly but don't know personally such as the cashier at the grocery store, people driving cars you never meet but who you share the road with, and of course those people we see and don't like. In fact if we consider the capacity to love to be linked to the metaphorical size of our heart (images of the Grinch who stole Christmas come to mind) the heart only increases with use, and like any muscle the harder it works the bigger it gets. Therefore it is only when we are loving our enemies that we are able to really exercise our heart at its fullest capacity. I like to say that pets and babies are really good practice. Your heart naturally responds in a loving manner to these two cute, cuddly types of beings. But babies and (some) pets don't talk back. They don't do things to hurt you. They don't break your heart. The people you live and deal with are a different story. They have good and bad days. They have their own history and their own pain to contend with. They, like you, are living as best they can with what they have been given and it just doesn't flow smoothly and easily all of the time. This is where the Heart is needed the most. It is no great accomplishment to love someone who is loving you back. It is the most difficult and therefore the greatest accomplishment to love someone who is hating or hurting you.

To quote the coach in the film "A League of Their Own," when the main character was complaining "it's too hard," he replies, "You love it because it's hard. If it was easy anyone could do it."[11] And so the challenge to rise up to the "big leagues" is before us. Many of us play a small game with small hearts because it is easier. Keeping your heart open and loving is a challenge. But there you have it; you've only got so much time to be here, in this body with this heartbeat. Sooner or later you will be gone and the opportunity to grow your heart will be gone too.

WHEN WILL THIS END?

As an astrologer, I very often counsel people who are going through a difficult time. Typically a Pluto or Uranus transit that has them feeling unnecessarily challenged, put upon, disheartened or disenchanted. And very often I'm asked, "When will this be over?" And of course the answer is – it's never over. We live with the consequences of our choices and actions for the rest of our lives. The best opportunities we have for growing are when things are difficult, when the chips are down. If, when someone is hating/hurting/attacking you, when that person is in your face, when in that very moment the urge to respond in-kind is strongest, you find you are able to remain in contact with your heart and allow yourself to be guided by it, you have grown. At that point you are literally emanating the power and strength that you have generated by accomplishing this most difficult of tasks. The heart is in the center of the Chakra system – in other words it is Command Central. When we honor the heart and allow it to run the show rather than allow our thoughts and emotions to usurp the chain of command we feel the power that comes from remaining centered and acting from a place of balance.

PAIRS

As mentioned in chapter 4, the Heart is the bridge where spirit and matter symbolically cross over and influence each other. And the pairing that I have mentioned in the last three chapters is now active. The more selfish aspects of the lower Chakras retreat as the awareness of our commonality – a shared source as well as a shared Planet – modifies their expression. The strength of the Warrior is applied in Service to others. The Passion and creativity of the Goddess is channeled into relationships and activities that have value to ourselves and others. The forms and institutions of Saturn and the stability of the Solar Plexus sustain the growth and evolution of us all. In connecting with the Physical dimension, the Spiritual impulses of the Crown Chakra now have a canvas to paint their visions upon. The intuitive faculty of the Brow Chakra facilitates sensitivity, compassion and understanding in our relationships. The immense power of our mind is brought to focus upon the knowledge, experience and skill needed to craft our unique Temple – our unique housing for our unique expression of spirit.

The circuit is now complete and each of our pairs – 1/7, 2/6, 3/5 – is connected and the true purpose of being alive – operating with all 7 energy centers active and participating in each thought, word and action – may be realized. And with a bit of math (the language of God according to Galileo) we see that each pair adds up to the number 8 – the symbol of infinity. The Radiance

Sutras say "within this very body are many gateways to the *Infinite*, where Incarnation and Immortality consummate their passion for each other." It is this *consummation* that is the marriage of your upper and lower chakras – your Spiritual and your material nature.

This, ultimately, is the reason for spirit to inhabit a body – so that spirit may accomplish something on the physical plane. "Bringing Heaven to Earth" is one way to put it. The Radiance Sutras illustrate how Spirit and Matter – Incarnation and Immortality – are passionately craving each other. One without the other is like having a right side without a left – incomplete and dysfunctional.

HEAVEN AND EARTH

Earth exists so that Heaven may be made manifest. They are not two separate 'places'. They are the two halves of the whole. The evidence of how life turns out when one or one's culture collectively is not in touch with the heart is painfully evident – in the lives of individuals and in the history of nations. Jesus said "the Kingdom of Heaven is within". All we really have to do is acknowledge its presence, honor its influence and choose to keep it at the center of our worldview. Not our passions or intellect – though of course they must play a significant role in our lives – but always in service to the center, the Heart, which must guide or steer the ship that is your Life.

CONCLUSION

The pairing of these upper/lower, physical/Spiritual energies is the key to realizing our Purpose, and the key lies in the Heart. If we look at Mercury's symbol, the Caduceus,

or the symbol for Kundalini (which is strikingly similar) with the two snakes twining up the spine we can see the number 8 replicated several times. The number 8 being the symbol for infinity, it is no coincidence that as you pair the numbers 1 and 7, 2 and 6, and 3 and 5, each combination adds up to 8. The "Gateways to the Infinite" must pair in order to achieve their potential – the bringing of Heaven to Earth. The key is encoded in the words themselves:

H-E-A-R-T

the offspring resulting from the consummation of the passion of

H-E-A-V-E-N and E-A-R-T-H.

PURPOSE

When I first started teaching this class, I called it "Purpose of Life 101." I believe this way of looking at a human being is the definitive start to realizing our purpose. As in *everyone's* purpose in the general sense. We are all created with these parts and this is what these parts do – therefore we are designed to do so and our Purpose is then known. The 26-word sentence may be used as a mantra at the start of day or a helpful reminder when one is off track, when we're having a bad day, or when faced with an existential crisis. Regardless how or when you use it, the essence – the boiled-down, central message of the Chakras – is that we are here to bring Heaven to Earth, via our Heart. This is what you are made for.

Bring It!

REFERENCES

1. Lorin Roche. *The Radiance Sutras* (Louisville, CO: Sounds True, 2014) Print.

2. Dan Brown. *The Da Vinci Code* (New York, NY: Doubleday, 2003) Print.

3. Kennedy, K., Marshall, F. & Molen, G. (Producers), Spielberg, S. (Director) (1991) *Hook* [Motion Picture] United States: Amblin

4. Pink Floyd. "Time" – Dark Side Of The Moon. Harvest. 1973. Record.

5. Eckhart Tolle. *A New Earth* (Penguin USA, 2005) Print.

6. Erich Fromm. *The Art of Loving* (New York, NY: Harper & Row, 1956) Print.

7. Michael H. Hart. *The 100: A Ranking of the Most Influential Persons in History* (New York, NY: Carol Publishing Group, 1992) Print.

8. Eckhart Tolle. *The Power of Now* (Vancouver, BC Canada: Namaste, 1997) Print.

9. Don Miguel Ruiz. *The Four Agreements* (San Rafael, CA: Amber-Allen, 1997) Print.

10. J.K. Rowling. H*arry Potter and the Half-Blood Prince* (New York, NY: Scholastic, 2005) Print.

11. Abbot, E. & Greenhut, R. (Producers), & Marshall, P. (Director). (1992). *A League of Their Own* [Motion Picture]. United States: Parkway Productions

Chakras, Mythology and Astrological Symbolism is presented world-wide as a 2-hour class. For tour dates and information on how to bring this presentation to your city please reach out to:

info@chakraoloyg.org

Johnny Barnett may be contacted for private astrological readings at info@chakraology.org

for further information, products, classes and astrological offerings please visit

www.Chakraology.org

Facebook.com/Chakraology

Instagram/Chakraology